ELSPETH TURNER grew up in the Scottish Borders. She held a senior lectureship in Economic and Social History at the University of Edinburgh and is returning in retirement to these and other storytelling roots after career shifts to facilitate equal access to higher education for school leavers – she was the first Director of Lothians Equal Access Programme for Schools and later a researcher and co-author in the field of Children's Rights with her husband, the late Stewart Asquith. She latterly worked for the Scottish Funding Council and lives in Edinburgh.

DONALD SMITH is a storyteller, novelist and playwright and founding Director of the Scottish Storytelling Centre. He was also a founder of the National Theatre of Scotland, for which he campaigned over a decade. Smith's non-fiction includes three previous *Journeys and Evocations*, co-authored with Stuart McHardy, *Freedom and Faith* on the Independence debate, and *Pilgrim Guide to Scotland* which recovers the nation's sacred geography. Donald Smith has written a series of novels, most recently *Flora McIvor*. He is currently Director of Traditional Arts and Culture Scotland.

The Tweed Dales

Journeys and Evocations

Exploring History, Folklore and Stories
from the Heart of the Scottish Borders

Elspeth Turner and Donald Smith

Luath Press Limited

EDINBURGH

www.luath.co.uk

First published 2017
Reprinted 2018
Reprinted 2019

ISBN: 978-1-912147-21-2

Printed and bound by
Bell & Bain Ltd., Glasgow

Typeset in 10.5 point Sabon and Din
by 3btype.com

Dedicated to

The late Nancy and
Hamish Turner and the bairns
of their Border bairns

and

David, Jean, Mary,
Pat and Nancy Smith,
children of Kirkurd Manse

Acknowledgements

The idea for this book was sparked by our involvement in the 'Seeing Stories' project which explored links between landscape features and stories connected with them in four European regions. The choice of the river Tweed catchment was an obvious one not least because the Scottish Borders was so fortunate in their recorders and interpreters, most notably James Hogg, Sir Walter Scott and Robert Chambers. In modern times, John Veitch's *History and Poetry of the Scottish Border*, W. S. Crockett's *The Scott Country*, Walter Elliot's *The New Minstrelsy of the Scottish Border 1805–2005*, and Alastair Moffat's *The Scottish Borders* have all added to the treasury, and we acknowledge our debt to the insights and materials collected by their authors and to those to whom they were indebted. Amongst the storytellers past and present, John Wilson, Sir George Douglas, Andrew Lang, John Buchan, Winifred M. Petrie, Jean Lang, and, in our own day, James Spence, Walter Elliot and Charlie Robertson have kept the tales of the Tweed Dales flowing.

Our thanks too to the poets who, inspired by the landscape, lore and history of the area, gave us a wealth of evocative words with which to illustrate the journeys. We thank Tim Douglas, Mhairi Owens, Isabella Johnstone, Dorcas Symms and Catriona Porteous for permission to quote their work and Will H Ogilvie's trustees for permission to quote his. Among the song makers we thank Eric Bogle for permission to quote from his original composition 'No Man's Land', and Janette McGinn for permission to quote from her late husband Matt McGinn's song 'The Rolling Hills of the Border'. Last but not least, thanks to the many who shared information, memories and stories with us, to Fiona Melrose and, for his assistance with photographs, Gordon Melrose.

Contents

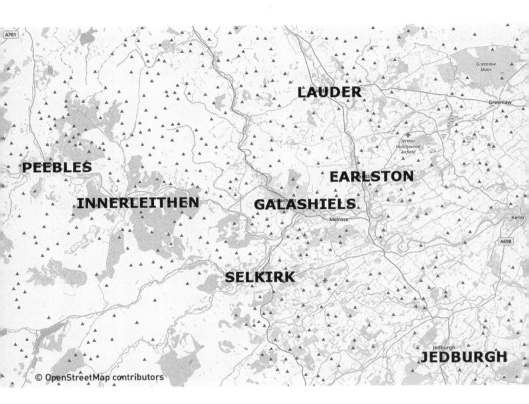

Introduction

The Scottish Borders lie between the Moorfoot and Lammermuir Hills to the north, and the Cheviot Hills and England to the south. People born and raised in this part of Scotland have a mindset that is neither Scottish nor English. They are Borderers. Their outlook and experience is as distinctive as the landscape and its geographical position within mainland Britain. These have their origins in geological events and are the context for the ebb and flow of people bringing new ways of seeing and doing things.

The landscape and the tussles for political, economic and spiritual control influenced how Borderers understood their world, and also their cultural and spiritual experience. Indeed, the landscape and its topographic features had a profound influence on the minds of the many visionaries, mystics, writers, thinkers, innovators and artists who came from or were inspired by this area.

There was a particular fascination with hills and rivers. Hilltops, especially those with wide vistas or panoramic views, are important to invaders and defenders of any land, and also have an influence on how travellers experience it. Hills look different depending on the angle of approach – and the means by which you approach them: on foot, by horse, by train, car or plane. All the hills of volcanic origin in the Borders look small seen first from high ground north, west or south of them. But they grow and change colour when you travel, as the early settlers did, down into the river valleys to reach them. The hill that looks like one hill can become two or three as your angle of approach changes and even, as the Eildon Hills do, four.

This shape-shifting quality, and the fact that people raised animals and took them to high summer pastures, might explain why hills feature so prominently in Border folk tales and legends. Hills are where fairies live, where sleeping armies rest, where the membrane between this and other worlds is thinnest, and where people disappear. These stories have their origins in the beliefs of the earliest settlers for whom the shape of the landscape was important. They revered nature, the land and trees.

Sometime later, the spiritual focus of the early farmers switched to celestial beings and the changing of the seasons. It took many generations and the development of religious institutions for monotheistic Christian beliefs to first overlap and then overtake primeval belief systems in the Scottish Borders. As late as the 13th century, the learned men of Europe believed not only in the existence of stars and planets but also in the predictive power of astrology. They combined knowledge of the physical world and the healing power of plants with alchemy and the presumed magical properties of substances. It was said that one such individual journeyed overnight on a flying horse to carry out diplomatic missions. Another claimed to have spent seven years with the fairies beneath the Eildon Hills and returned with the gift of prophecy. We meet Michael Scot and Thomas the Rhymer later.

There was magic in the hills but there was also something in the water. The river Tweed brought water and people together as it headed for the North Sea. Rivers loom large in Border history, legend, story and ballad. Until roads and railways snaked across the landscape, the easiest way to travel was along river valleys. As the towns of today bear witness, junctions of rivers were convenient places to trade goods and to meet for ceremonial events. Water has a special and enduring place in rituals and spiritual beliefs, while the junctions of rivers were associated with movement between one world and the next. Rivers and their banks also feature prominently in tales of family honour with their avenged and ill-fated lovers. The Tweed and its tributaries played a big part in shaping the outlook and mindset of Borderers.

However, the river was, until fairly recently, also a barrier. Bridges across the Tweed were few until the 18th century as were, for much of its length, places it could be forded safely. This effectively split the area in two: the lands north of the river and the lands to the south. There were also significant differences in how people saw and did things in the western, middle and eastern sections of the Tweed. People had a sense of belonging to a particular tributary or stretch of the Tweed each with its own character, set in a distinctive landscape with its own river of stories and creative outpourings. These have trickled down to us and are continually added to in spoken, written, musical, theatrical and visual forms – and sometimes all of them at once. Threads of ancient and more recent belief systems blend to create a richly textured story in much the same way as raw wool is transformed into the woollen textiles for which the Scottish Borders are famed.

The distinctive blend of emotions and responses each landscape stirs up are echoed in stories filtered through the voices of storytellers, the pens of poets and historians, and the tools of artists and crafters. We hope you will experience these too, as you journey with us through the landscape.

The Journeys

The six circular journeys are designed to give you a glimpse into the experiences and outlook of people in six distinctive landscapes. The routes described are for people with wheels of some kind. And like a wheel, journeys 2 to 6 are spokes radiating from the hub of journey 1. There are however many places travellers might want to abandon their wheels and take to the hills or the river bank. The Land Reform (Scotland) Act 2003 opened up access to the countryside in Scotland, but there are a few limitations as set out in the Scottish Outdoor Access Code of 2005 (www.outdooraccess-scotland.com).

The journeys follow the roads network, but intersect at various points with cross-country walking and cycle routes which pass through the area. Whilst road directions are correct at date of publication, things change so do take along a current map. Detailed guides for the Border Abbeys Way, the Southern Upland Way, the St Cuthbert's Way, the Sir Walter Scott Way, the John Buchan Way, local walks around towns and some villages, and opening hours of visitor attractions are readily available from visitor information centres and online.

The journeys can be done in any order and explorers can join a route at any point and slip between them as time, mood, interests and weather suggest. All journeys are however described and mileages measured with a start and end point at Tweedbank Station, the terminus (for now) of the newly restored Borders Railway Waverley line running from Edinburgh. For rendezvousing purposes, nearby Abbotsford, the quirky home of master storyteller Sir Walter Scott, is equally suitable.

Each journey is prefaced by a brief introduction outlining key influences, historical events and people to set the scene.

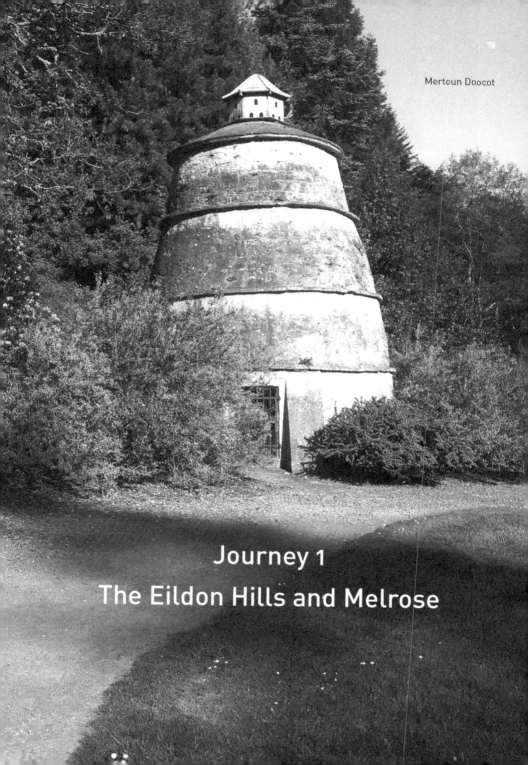

Mertoun Doocot

Journey 1

The Eildon Hills and Melrose

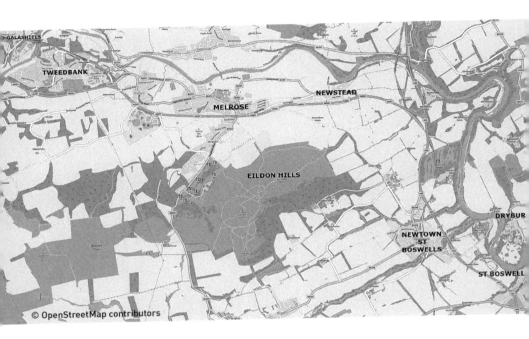

© OpenStreetMap contributors

Halfway between the Cheviot Hills on the English border and Edinburgh on the other side of the Lammermuir Hills, the river Tweed runs like a glittering zip along the subterranean join between the uplands to the north and the undulating lands to the south. Having travelled through hard grey silurian rocks to the west, the river meets softer red sandstone and limestone rocks and heads east on a winding course through a fertile river plain to the sea. Standing guard over this natural crossroads in the ancient landscape, with its iconic trio of manmade bridges, is the northernmost Eildon Hill, a haunting and haunted legacy of a volcano which woke up then fell asleep unwitnessed. Where better to sense how the Border landscape must have looked and felt to the procession of peoples who came into the Tweed valley?

Here we meet the Selgovae, a Celtic British Iron Age tribe and their neighbours to the east, the Votadini. They left no written records but built an impressive hilltop enclosure on the North Eildon. We meet the Romans who built their Scottish headquarters at the foot of the North Eildon. They came and went several times between 79 CE and around 220 CE. They left the Celtic tribes with an impressive road network, and the task of establishing a new power balance in the area.

Then came the Anglo-Saxon Northumbrians and, with them, the English language, Christianity and the first abbeys. Eventually the Kingdom of Northumbria stretched as far north as the Firth of Forth but over the 11th century the Scots won back some of the land. For a brief time, the Tweed was the new frontier. But then the Normans crossed the English Channel in 1066, swept north to subjugate the Kings of Northumbria and, by marrying into the Scottish royal family in the early 12th century, gained power in Scotland. This was not a conquest, but the Normans brought new ways of doing things which continue to this day to influence how Borderers live.

From the days of David I, Scotland's monarchs had three priorities: to secure and defend the border; to order the day to day and spiritual lives of the people; and to develop Scotland's economy, so gathering funds for their own projects. Achieving the first priority involved granting land to nobles, many of them Anglo Normans, in return for a pledge to provide a set number of fighting men as the king required. The second was achieved by reforming the law, establishing a second wave of abbeys and creating the parish structure to serve secular as well as ecclesiastical administration. And the third was achieved by land grants which generated rent paid for by sales of crops, animals and their produce; by setting up burghs and licensing them to hold markets; and by taxing the flow of goods and services. Capitalism had arrived!

The new system opened up opportunities for Borderers, while the pressure on nobles to meet their obligations to the monarch had some unintended consequences. Nobles were responsible for protecting the families of those who owed them military service. As well as vying for power and influence by courting royal favour, and making judicious marriages, many of the most powerful families between the Tweed and the Cheviots had, by the 15th century, taken to reiving. That is, they were helping themselves to their rivals' assets, usually the cattle they relied on for food. Long running feuds with neighbours and even relatives became a way of life, despite the human cost in lost lives and loves.

This state of affairs arose directly from the uncertainties of living near a politically unstable frontier. In order to make life for his Border subjects less uncertain or, as he put it, to 'make the key keep the castle and the bracken bush keep the cow' King James I ordered the wealthiest landholders to build tower houses and they willingly obliged. A second wave followed a century later after Henry VIII of England had ordered his nobles to build tower houses 'for resisting the Scottis men'. Towers however served their defensive purpose rather too well as far as royalty were concerned, because some of their owners regarded themselves as above the law and beyond royal authority. Paradoxically, the exchange of land for military service became the means by which the Border Reivers wielded considerable power and threatened Scotland's economic and political stability. Attempts by successive monarchs to 'daunton' them had only temporary success, because the rulers' inability to protect those close to a contested border meant local families continued to put their own people and interests first. They literally *had* to fight for their lives. The reiving culture therefore persisted until conditions in the area changed with the Union of the Crowns in 1603.

People living around the Eildons generally suffered less from English attempts to regain Scotland than those closer to the border, but the 16th century was a distressing and uncertain time. Terrible damage was inflicted by English troops, especially during Henry VIII of England's 'rough wooing' of the 1540s. This brutal attack was triggered by Scotland's refusal to marry the infant Mary Queen of Scots to his infant son. And there was religious upheaval when, during the Scottish Reformation, Roman Catholicism was outlawed, the abbeys closed their doors and Presbyterian Calvinism became the only spiritual creed to which people could publicly profess.

The local population carried on as best they could. The whirring of spinning wheels and the clacking of handlooms became everyday sounds from the second half of the 17th century but the technological revolution which later mechanised textile-making processes largely bypassed this part of the borders. The area was also on the fringes of major changes in agriculture in the 18th and 19th centuries. Perhaps this is why the stories of past peoples, their ways of life and thinking and their stories seem particularly close to the surface in this area. It is a good place to start our journey.

As we travel through this landscape we meet a monk who averted a famine, a Scot and a Scott – one a multilingual wizard, the other a wizard with words. And we hear how a heart came home alone, how a horse trader got more than he bargained for, and how two scheming monks were outwitted.

The Journey: 32 miles

From Tweedbank Station turn left at roundabout (signed Melrose), follow signs for A68 (signed Edinburgh/Jedburgh), take first exit at roundabout (signed Edinburgh) and proceed to Leaderfoot viewpoint.

The Romans were greeted by the striking sight of three hills outlined on the horizon as they approached for the first time and went on to name their Scottish headquarters Trimontium ('three hills'). A short walk up the disused road running parallel to the river takes us to a monument on the site of the camp and a series of viewing platforms with information boards. Just imagine sitting with two or three thousand others in the most northerly amphitheatre of the Roman Empire watching the Roman equivalent of Edinburgh's Military Tattoo.

The Romans were not the first to make their mark on this landscape. The Celtic British hilltop enclosure on North Eildon was the largest of its kind in Scotland and, like Trimontium, seems to have been used intermittently. It latterly consisted of 300 or so huts which probably housed the crowds who gathered periodically to pay taxes, attend political gatherings or celebrate the turning of the seasons. Fires lit on Eildon Hill North are visible from much of the Tweed valley so when the Anglo-Saxon Northumbrians arrived they named the hills 'the Aeled-dun', meaning firehill.

Leaving Leaderfoot turn right and, at roundabout, take second exit onto A6091 (signed Galashiels, Melrose) then first right onto B6361 (signed Newstead).

Newstead is the oldest continuously inhabited village in Scotland. The numerous wells archaeologists have discovered here – more than 200 – tell us that the area was already pretty crowded when the Romans arrived. Everyone who lived here relied on these wells for fresh water. During the Bronze and Iron Ages, metal workers fashioned a variety of items here, some of which became offerings to the gods or goddesses associated with particular wells, springs or pools. Quite why some wells had a spiritual significance while others did not is a mystery but the

Romans too, when they closed the wells supplying Trimontium, had their priests appease the water gods with animal and metal offerings such as swords or shields. The stories and legends of pre-Christian Anglo Saxon times are full of watery tales, and the holy wells, so important to early and later Christians, were often sited at places with earlier spiritual associations.

Proceed to Melrose and park.

Newstead was home to the masons who built the 12th century abbey in Melrose. Later we visit Old Mailros, the site of an abbey built six centuries earlier a couple of miles downstream, but we are greeted now by the rosy ruins of Melrose Abbey. This second abbey was founded by David I, the reforming king, in 1136. The Cistercian monks, brought from Riveaulx in Yorkshire, came with a mission to contemplate, grow things, convert the locals and pray for their souls. They were also record keepers, and the Abbey became famous for learning and the production of books. Much of what we know about this area's early history comes from the Chronicle of Melrose. Begun in 1140, it pieces together the history of the first abbey at Old Mailros and goes on to document the story of this abbey until 1270. Stories about the monks were of course also told by local people. The most memorable ascribe the achievements of religious men to their ability to work miracles and see visions. Such tales reflect belief in a spiritual cosmos, though one with often practical implications.

Monks and Miracle Workers

Drythelm, a venerable monk at Mailros, was given to visions and seeings. But he had not always been a man of religion. Earlier in his life, he had fallen ill, so ill in fact that that those tending him gave him up for dead. The next morning however they found him not only awake but with an amazing tale to tell about his travels through the realm of the spirits.

He had, he said, been guided along a path by a heavenly being clothed in shining light with, on one side, blazing fires and, on the other, freezing snows. The souls of mankind were, he saw, being tossed from one extreme to the other. Eventually Drythelm was led into a place of total darkness and silence and left alone but presently his guide reappeared in the form of a star which led him into open light and towards a wall endless in its dimensions and without doors or windows. As they approached, Drythelm was suddenly transported atop the wall and found himself looking down into a meadow full of flowers and lush grasses through which people in white robes wandered at their ease.

Drythelm returned from this journey to bodily consciousness and recovered to tell his story and indeed to become a monk and to devote the rest of his life to ascetic prayer and meditations. He also bathed daily in the Tweed whatever the weather, refusing afterwards to dry his robe. One time, when he was bobbing amidst ice on the river, Drythelm was asked how he could endure such cold, to which he replied shortly, 'I have felt worse cold', remembering less Borders winters than the frozen wastes of the underworld.

And Waltheof (Walter), the second abbot of Melrose (who just happened to be David I's stepson), was said to have miraculously saved around 4000 starving people. When the harvest failed, more and more desperate people came to camp in the fields and woods around the Abbey hoping the monks would share what food they had with them. Walter did not fail them. He ordered that the grain in the Abbey's granaries be distributed until it ran out. The monks in charge of the stores reckoned that there was only enough to last for two weeks but somehow the supplies lasted three months, just long enough for the next year's grain to ripen and be gathered.

Any doubts that Walter could work miracles were set aside when, 11 years after his death in 1159, his coffin was opened and his body was as fresh as the day it was buried. It was opened again 36 years later and again 34 years after that. On both occasions, it was recorded that there were no signs of decay.

Quite why Abbot Walter's body did not decompose defies scientific explanation. However, whilst he may have had divine assistance to stave off famine, he could also have supplemented the grain with other food stored by the monks including apples from the Abbey's vast orchards. Descendants of these very apple trees are still grown in Priorwood

Gardens in Melrose. The Abbey also owned more than 5,000 acres of pasture and woodland spread across Lauderdale, Ettrick and Tweeddale. By 1300 this abbey alone was producing five per cent of all Scottish wool and exporting most of it to Northern Europe. The monks themselves took no part in the day to day running of the Abbey's enterprises but relied on the labour of 'lay brothers' whose lives were hard compared with the monks, and local labour working under one master or another.

The wealth and political power of the abbeys however made them a target in troubled times. And in the Abbey's early years, the monks brought trouble to their own door. Scuffles with neighbouring ecclesiastics were not unknown, for example in 1269 when the Abbot of Melrose and some monks attacked properties in Wedale belonging to the Bishop of St Andrews. They were excommunicated for killing one man and wounding others and, we presume, expelled from the Abbey.

Indeed, although monks were exempt from providing the military service other landholders owed the king, the Melrose monks donned armour and sallied forth with the Abbot's blessing to fight the cause of a Scottish King. They rode out, for example, for Robert the Bruce which prompted an enraged Edward I to order the destruction of the Abbey in 1322. It was rebuilt with a grant from Robert the Bruce when he became king. Inconveniently for Scotland's finances, the grant far exceeded the money in the Scots treasury at the time but Robert honoured his pledge and the Abbey was rebuilt, only to be attacked by Richard II in 1385. He however felt so bad about it afterwards that he gave money to rebuild! The masons brought in to repair the damage added gargoyles of a fat monk and a pig playing the bagpipes, suggesting not only that they had a free hand in embellishing the building but also that they were not Scots.

The Abbey was attacked a final time in 1545. By then the efforts of a succession of popes to persuade the monks of this and other monasteries to honour their vows and live frugally had clearly failed as these lines from that time sadly suggest:

The monks of Melrose made good kail,
On Fridays when they fasted
They wanted neither beef nor ale
As long as their neighbours' lasted.

Not long after the final assault on the walls of Melrose Abbey, all Roman Catholic institutions were swept aside in the Reformation, the doors of the Abbey closed and the buildings were left to crumble.

And so, this abbey lay being raided for building stone by townspeople until Sir Walter Scott spearheaded the first campaign to rescue it. He wrote:

If thou wouldst view fair Melrose aright,
Go visit it by the pale moonlight;
For the gay beams of lightsome day
Gild, but to flout, the ruins gray.
When the broken arches are black in night,
And each shafted oriel glimmers bright,
When the cold light's uncertain shower
Streams on the ruined central tower...
When distant Tweed is heard to rave,
And the owlet to hoot o'er the dead man's grave,
Then go – but go alone the while –
Then view St David's ruined pile.

Scott later confessed that he never had seen it by moonlight but those who have followed his instruction bear no grudge. John Geddie said of Melrose Abbey that it is 'memorable even more for its legendary and literary associations than for its actual history'. And perhaps it is.

King Robert the Bruce, alongside whom the soldier monks of Melrose fought and who regained Scotland's independence, found eternal rest in Melrose Abbey... or at least, his heart did.

The Heart of Robert the Bruce

'A noble heart may have nane ease gif freedom fail', are the words inscribed near Bruce's heart at Melrose. These words are from the chivalrous epic of John Barbour, following the famous lines:

> A! Freedome is a noble thing!
> Freedome makes man to have liking:
> Freedome all solace to man givis:
> He livis at ease that freely livis!

Barbour's 'Brus' is concerned as much with the King's knightly virtues as his political and military struggles. Bruce had sworn that if he escaped death in the wars to keep Scotland free, he would go on pilgrimage or crusade to Jerusalem. But age and illness thwarted his desire so his dying wish was that his heart be taken to the Holy Land. Sir James Douglas, another of Barbour's knightly heroes, was entrusted with this sacred task. However, he was killed en route, fighting the Saracens in Spain. According to Barbour:

> The good lord Douglas pressed the enemy so hard
> they fled in disarray, and Douglas gave pursuit
> as a hunter leads the pack, with William Saintclair
> the gallant knight of Roslin.
> But when the Saracen saw how few were in the band,
> not more than ten in number, they rallied with main force,
> closing round the knights. Seeing Saintclair surrounded
> like to fall, Sir James tore the casket from his neck-
> 'To Bruce, to Bruce!' he cries – hurls the heart into the host
> and follows to the fray.

Douglas was himself killed but his body and the casket containing the heart of Robert the Bruce were brought back and Bruce's heart buried in Melrose Abbey.

Melrose Abbey was built on the edge of a village called Fordel – a place to ford the river – which later took the Abbey's name and grew into a town. The annual Eve of St John torchlight procession of masons from the Lodge of St John around the Abbey is a fitting reminder that the town owes its existence to the Abbey and its masons.

The Abbey was one of Scotland's four principal places of medieval devotion, bringing pilgrims from near and far. Melrose consequently became a political as well as a spiritual meeting place. The great and the good (or not so good) gathered here to sign documents and treaties such as the 1424 Treaty of Melrose which James I hoped would bring to heel members of the Douglas family, by then a particular threat to his authority.

Melrose fell on hard times after the Abbey closed in the middle of the 16th century. During the following century, however the town became a major producer of linen cloth, much of it destined for distant markets. When demand for linen collapsed with the coming of cotton, Melrose tried with only temporary success to compete effectively in the making of cotton and woollen cloth. The mechanised production methods of the first industrial revolution however needed fast running rivers and the middle-aged Tweed was not a contender. So when Catherine Spence left Melrose for Australia with her family at the age of 14 in 1839, she left it at a low ebb. By the time she returned to visit in 1865 as one of that country's foremost social reformers, an advocate for women and children and a champion of equality, the fortunes of the town had revived, thanks in no small part to Sir Walter Scott. People flocked to Abbotsford, the ruined Abbey and other sites mentioned in his poems and novels particularly after the coming of the railway in 1849. This compact and peaceful little town punched well above its weight. And, being the home of seven-a-side rugby and the renowned Borders Book Festival, it still does.

We cannot leave Melrose without mention of the wizard Michael Scot who, as Walter Scott recounted in his epic poem, 'The Lay of the Last Minstrel', is said to be buried in Melrose Abbey with his Book of Magic. One of many stories of how Michael Scot used his wizardry credits him with causing three hills to be created from one.

Michael Scot and the Eildon Hills

The story goes that the Devil sent three demons to distract Michael Scot from using his skills and magical powers for good ends. They had come, they said, to help him but it was not long before Michael figured out what they were up to. Getting them to leave, however, proved to be quite a challenge. In the end, he came up with the idea of setting them an impossible task.

And so, one night, he sent them off to create three Eildons from what was then one hill. Michael was sure that would keep them occupied for ever! In the morning however they were back having completed the task in a single night. The next task Michael set them was to throw a kerb of stone across the River Tweed. Surely, thought Michael, the flowing water would thwart their attempts. But yet again they returned having completed the job, some say at Ednam, some say at Kelso.

Finally, after many more unsuccessful attempts to get rid of them, he sent them off to the coast to make ropes from sand... and there they still are some say, unable to complete the task because, of course, the sea washes away their efforts twice a day.

There are in fact four Eildons. Little Eildon is what remains of the neck of the volcano. But the legend said three so three it has been ever since. We of course know how old these hills are and when humans arrived in the area. But that knowledge is recent and this story was once as plausible an explanation of how this exceptional cluster of hills came to be as any other, especially if you believed Michael Scot lived a long life, as wizards do.

Michael Scot also had a reputation for prophesy. That was not unusual in medieval Europe. Some, like local men Drythelm and Cuthbert, devoted themselves to the monastic life after they had visions they believed were sent by God. It was also common belief that the future could be read in the stars. Quite how Michael Scot's prophesies came to him we don't know but some of them were uncannily accurate. For example, he warned the Holy Roman Emperor Frederick II that he would die near a city associated with the Roman goddess Flora. Frederick avoided Florence after that... but died at

Fiorentina, a town also associated with Flora. Scot even prophesied his own death from a stone falling on his head and, despite his efforts to avoid that fate, it seems that was what carried him off.

Darnick Tower

Born in the Tweed valley in the 1170s, Michael Scot was in fact one of Europe's most learned men in his day. He lived and worked at one time or another in Oxford, Paris, Palermo, Salerno and Toledo and mixed with people who were the pioneers of their time in scientific discoveries, mathematics, medicine and philosophy. Michael was educated by monks and took holy orders before becoming the mediaeval equivalent of a modern academic. Having mastered multiple languages, he also worked as a translator and adviser to the Holy Roman Emperor Frederick II and Popes Innocent IV and Gregory IX. Indeed, he is credited with reintroducing Aristotle's writings to European readers by translating them from Arabic, the only language in which some survived. Such was his detailed knowledge of human biology that he was commissioned to write manuals and he happened to be in Salerno and Toledo when the alchemists, the forefathers of modern chemistry, discovered how to distil alcohol. If he brought back this knowledge and used it in preparing his medicines, we have him to thank for hangovers and for the later whisky industry.

So why is this clever man remembered more for his prophesies and his supernatural feats than his academic achievements? One reason may be that Michael seemed pretty eccentric in the eyes of his Tweedside neighbours. He was said, for example, to wear strange clothes and to have fed guests on food spirited from the royal kitchens of Spain and France. And a story got around that he had travelled to Rome and back, a journey that took others weeks, in a single night. His purpose in going was to find out the date of Shrove Tuesday, a date relevant to establishing the date of Easter which fell differently each year. He had probably learned how the date was worked out while he was in Italy, but it was said that he had travelled there and back on a big black horse which he had traded for his shadow and flew faster than the wind or an unspoken thought between lovers. We will never know but perhaps some of the stories told and retold about the superhuman exploits of Michael Scot the Wizard came from the mouth of the man himself.

And what of the Book of Magic that is said to be buried with Michael Scot? Might this have been a manuscript written in Arabic script? Dante, and later, Walter Scott, are responsible for Michael's portrayal in literature as a master of the dark arts. Dante was writing 70 years after Michael Scot's death at a time when the Roman Catholic Church was less tolerant of pre-Christian practices and the eighth crusade against the Moors (Muslims) had just ended with the loss of Jerusalem. The fact that Michael, besides being a 'false prophet' according to Dante, was a translator of Arabic writings and had worked for Frederick II, whose tolerant attitude to Muslims and Jews upset the Popes of his day, may explain the hostility. Walter Scott's later portrayal of Michael in the 'Lay of the last Minstrel' only compounded his dark reputation. The making and breaking of reputations by the written media is no recent phenomenon! Whatever the truth about this clever, enquiring man, he was already a mystery and a legend in his own time.

Proceed to Darnick past Melrose rugby ground and at Y junction take left onto High Cross Avenue (signed Darnick).

Darnick is, as the winding road hints, an old settlement. Two of Darnick's original three towers survive, Fishers Tower as a ruin and Darnick Tower, a fine 16th century tower house, as a private residence. A teenage James V took refuge here during the Battle of Melrose Bridge in 1526. This battle later became known as Skirmish Field to distinguish it from the Battle of Melrose in 1378. On that earlier occasion, a Douglas defeated English troops who had pursued his men from Berwick upon Tweed.

Skirmish Field

A skirmish means a small battle but that is a relative term in the Borders. This fracas also involved the Douglases, supported by the Maxwells and the Kers. The Earl of Angus, chief of the House of Douglas, had the young King James V (his stepson) in guardianship when they came to Jedburgh to hold a Justice Court. But the teenage King was chafing at his confinement and sent a secret message to Sir Walter Scott of Branxholm and Buccleuch, the renowned Borders scrapper 'Wicked Wat', taking up an offer to rescue him.

Acting on this, Walter Scott accompanied by 600 men intercepted the Earl of Angus's much smaller party on their way north with James. James was quickly got out of harm's way and watched impatiently from the battlements of Darnick Tower to see which side would prevail. He saw the attacking band of Scots and Eliots get the upper hand and no doubt thought his dream of being free to rule in his own right was about to come true. But then a substantial band of Kerrs and Armstrongs, who had earlier left the royal escort, returned and James's would-be rescuers fled the field, having killed around 100 of the Earl of Angus's supporters but lost around 80 of their own. At a spot later marked by the Turn

Again stone, one of Scott's men, James Elliot, turned back on their pursuers and stabbed the leader of the Kerrs.

The King, subdued and frustrated, travelled on to Edinburgh leaving behind a death to be avenged – as 26 years later it was when the Kerrs killed Walter Scott in the High Street of Edinburgh. This feud continued with considerable loss of life on both sides until, finally, a diplomatic marriage ended hostilities.

This bloody event was one of many incidents which sparked the family feuds and lawlessness that plagued the borders between the 13th and the 16th centuries. James V did however shrug off the controlling hand of the Earl of Angus two years later and immediately got down to sorting out the dire state Scotland's finances had got into following the Battle of Flodden. He struck a deal with Pope Paul II which led to Scotland adopting a legal and judicial system based on different principles to the common law system the Normans had rolled out over England and Scotland. It is a system which survives to this day. No small achievement for a teenager!

Leaving Darnick turn left at T junction onto A7 (signed Galashiels) and follow signs to Abbotsford OR for optional walk to Skirmish Field, turn first right from A7 (signed Gattonside) and first left to park, returning to A7 to proceed to Abbotsford.

On the south bank of the Tweed sits Abbotsford, the home of the literary giant Sir Walter Scott. Denied his wish to buy Darnick Tower, Walter Scott purchased Cartleyhole in 1811, renamed it Abbotsford, demolished the old farmhouse and built a new house to his own design. This incorporated several historic architectural styles. The result was what he described as 'a conundrum castle'.

Scott was a veritable magpie. He filled Abbotsford with 'found' objects which included bits of the ruined Melrose Abbey, parts of Edinburgh's original mercat cross and the 16th century door of Edinburgh's Tolbooth or jail (the Heart of Midlothian). The house at Abbotsford is a compendium of story and legend in stone. The contents reflect Walter Scott's approach to writing both his poetry and novels, and to gathering

Border folktales and ballads in *Minstrelsy of the Scottish Borders*. He had a talent for weaving together historical facts, folk tales and ballads with strands of romance and pathos to create works, which, like his house, melded in a unique style which both revered and sometimes rode rough shod over the past and its traditions.

Like other Romantic writers of the period, Scott portrayed the landscape in which historical events took place in vivid detail. This heightened the literary drama and led visitors to these locations to view them in emotional terms. In doing this he took his cue from the old ballads he collected which, with their rich descriptions, gave places as well as people characters. Scott was not only responsible for inventing modern tourism but also for pioneering historical fiction in world literature.

Return to A6091, follow signs for A68 and turn right at the sign for the Rhymers Stone.

This takes us to a viewpoint over Melrose, Trimontium and the Tweed. These hills witnessed many battles. It is said that Arthur and the Knights of the Round Table fought a battle on or near the Eildon and that Arthur had a base here. Rival claimants to the Northumbrian throne also fought a three-day battle here in 762.

It is no surprise that the Eildons, steeped in history and lying beneath a multi-layered quilt of Christian and pre-Christian beliefs, have a prominent place in Border legends. Indeed, if the many stories are to be believed, it is pretty crowded under the Eildons. Legend has it that they are hollow hills and that there exists beneath the rocks, grass and heather, otherworlds. Arthur is, for example, said to be sleeping with his knights and their horses beneath Lucken hare or Lucken Howe (the Little Eildon) awaiting the Doomsday bugle call that will waken them and spur them into action.

Canonbie Dick

There was once a famous horse dealer from the borderlands of Scotland and England; they called him Dick, Canonbie Dick. One night he stayed late at St Boswells Fair, dealing and drinking before setting off with the magnificent white stallion he had bought that day to get to his lodgings on the far side of the Eildons.

Suddenly a dark figure appeared on the track in front of him, cloaked and with a hat pulled low over his eyes.

'Dick, Canonbie Dick?' the figure spoke.

'Aye, that's me.'

'What will you take for your horse, Dick?'

'Oh it's not for sale, magnificent beast, light of my eye...'

The man held out a small leather bag – Dick heard the clink and saw the chink of gold – a hundred golden guineas.

'Will this be sufficient?'

'Yes, indeed, well...' said Dick and before he could comment further, the black hooded figure took the bridle, turned and headed round the corner of the hill. 'Wait, stranger, strike the bargain...' shouted Dick as he followed the man round the corner. The man however had disappeared into the dark leaving Dick with his bag of gold, but no horse.

Dick trudged back to his lodgings but the next day he was back at the fair with his surplus funds and again he purchased a fine stallion. This time he deliberately went home round the hill holding his horse hopefully by the bridle. And sure enough, once again the cloaked figure appeared on the path, bid for the horse with the clink and chink of gold and Dick complied. But this time Dick, determined to know who the stranger was, tried to insist on going to an inn to seal the bargain as was the usual practice. To no avail. The man disappeared into the night leaving Dick puzzled but 100 guineas the richer.

So, on the third day he was quick to secure a third fine stallion and, as soon as dusk fell, he was on the road. And as on the previous two nights, the cloaked figure with the black hat pulled down low on his brow hailed him and bid for the horse – 100 golden guineas.

Dick again agreed but this time he was determined to go after the mysterious purchaser with the clinking chinking bags of gold so he said,

'If you won't go with me to the tavern to seal the bargain, stranger, let me go with you.' The figure turned back and stared at Dick from beneath his hat's brim.

'Are you sure, Dick, you want to come?'

'Aye, surely.'

'Then follow.'

So Dick followed him round the shoulder of the hill. Suddenly they were before an old doorway set in the hillside, all studded with metal nails. It swung open and Dick followed him, puzzled, since he had not seen that door before. Inside, the door opened into a long cavern reaching into the mountain. All down one side was a row of stalls, each with a white stallion standing quietly. One last stall was empty till the cloaked figure led his last purchase in to complete the row. On the other side was a series of stone slabs on each of which lay a knight in full armour, still as the grave. And at the far end of the cavern was a great stone table like an altar.

As Dick looked in amazement the hooded man went to the high table and swept off his hat to reveal flowing white locks and a long white beard.

'Aye, you know me now, Dick. You have come of your own free will and now you must make your choice.' He pointed to the table where lay a sword in its scabbard and beside it an old hunting horn. 'Now' said the cloaked figure, 'will you draw the sword or blow the horn?'

Dick hesitated in fear and astonishment. He could blow the horn or perhaps he should draw the sword. But what might happen – would he offend the sleeping warriors? He was not a man of violence but of cunning. Which to choose? He really didn't know but in the end lunged for the horn and blew. A wail of sound filled the cave, echoed and resounded. Candles guttered in a blast of wind. Horses reared and neighed and there was a clash of arms on stone. As Dick felt himself caught up in the wind a great shout roared through the blast.

'Cursed be the man who blew the horn when he should have drawn the sword.'

With a great cry, Dick was lifted by the howling gale, swept out of the cave and fell senseless on the hillside. There the next morning he was found, exposed and feverish. They carried him to an inn at Melrose where later that day he died, having related this strange and disturbing tale but without putting a name to the figure who made him choose between sword and horn. Surely this was Merlin, loyal servant of Arthur. Who else could convince the knights and their steeds that Dick's bugle blast was a false alarm?

And it was through another door in that same hill that, in the 13th century, the Faerie Queen led a young nobleman and one time bard to the Earls of Dunbar, to live in her kingdom for seven years.

Thomas and the Faerie Queen

Thomas of Ercildoune often went walking in the hills and on this particular day he had gone it was thought to the slopes of Eildon Hill North. He was resting in the shade of a tree when along came a beautiful woman riding a grey horse. The well-known ballad sets the scene:

> True Thomas lay on Huntly Bank
> A ferlie he spied wi his ee;
> And there he saw a lady bright
> Come riding doun by the Eildon Tree.
> Her shirt was o the grass-green silk,
> Her mantle o the velvet fine;
> At ilka tett of her horse's mane
> Hung fifty siller bells and nine.

To his surprise, she stopped and spoke to him. She was, she said, the queen of a far country and had come to find him. He asked her for a kiss, and she offered more, as a result of which he agreed to go with her to her faerie kingdom. She warned him however that whatever he saw or heard he must not speak. If he did, he could never return home.

And so, Thomas went with the Faerie Queen to her kingdom and said not a word until almost seven years had passed. Then, according to the oldest version of the ballad, the Fairie Queen tells him,

> 'Tomorrow the foul fiend o hell
> Will speir his fee
> An suth tae tell
> A meikle man, he wad chuse thee,
> But to you fause
> I shall not be.'

Thomas would have known that every seven years the faeries had to pay a tiend (tax) to the devil in the form of a human soul so not only had he had a pretty good motive for keeping quiet all that time but he also knew that one way or another he would be leaving the Faerie Queen. And so, they went to the Eildon hill entrance to her kingdom and, as they emerged into the world of day and night, he spoke

> 'That wi you I dwelt ladye
> Afore you wend awa, a token gie.'

And she replied,

> 'To harp or carp Thomas may chuse
> Tae spell or tailis tell
> An aye spak truth.'

And so, choosing the telling of tales in rhyme with a tongue that could not lie, Thomas took his leave of Huntly Bank and returned to Ercildoune to resume his old life but a life with a difference – he had the gift of prophecy.

That however was not the end of the story. Some years later Thomas disappeared again. This time he had witnesses. Thomas was eating dinner with friends at his tower house in Earlston when a servant rushed in to say that two deer had walked out of the forest that surrounded the tower and were just standing there. When the man went on to say that the deer were white and that one was a hart and the other a hind, Thomas leapt to his feet. This was surely a message from the Faerie Queen calling him back to her kingdom!

And so, Thomas left his meal and his friends, walked out of his tower house and followed the deer into the forest without a backward look leaving his old life behind for good.

A monument marks the alleged site of the Eildon Tree a five minute walk beyond the limit of the road for cars. The story of True Thomas, so named because he could not tell a lie, has had many tellings in many mediums since.

Return to A6091, turn right, take second exit at the roundabout (signed Jedburgh) then first left onto minor road with passing places (signed Old Melrose). Park for optional walk to Old Melrose.

Little physical evidence remains of Mailros Abbey established in 653 at a time when this area was ruled from Northumbria. A walk down the woodland path to the site is however worthwhile to get a feel for the surroundings in which Abbots Aidan, Boisil and Cuthbert, all later recognised as saints, lived with a handful of monks. As Dorothy Wordsworth said on visiting this peaceful riverside glade, 'We wished we could have brought the ruins of Melrose to this spot'.

Like most early Christian sites, Mailros Abbey was set up by monks on or near a place revered by the Celtic British tribes. King Oswald of Northumbria established it as a sister abbey to Lindisfarne on the Northumbrian coast after his prayers for success in battle were answered. While the names attached to other features in the area are Anglo Saxon and were probably given by Oswald's monks, the name Mailros is Cymric and older.

Oswald brought Aidan from Iona to be the first prior. He in turn brought Boisil who later admitted Cuthbert as a novice. Cuthbert was a local boy who became a monk after he had a vision of Abbot Aidan ascending to heaven on the night he died. He became the most famous saint of the Borderlands and was known as a man of gentleness and piety who eschewed wealth and status in favour of the villages and solitary retreats of his beloved Northumbria. He arrived at Old Mailros however on a horse bearing a spear and he seems to have had a reputation as a battle saint, dispensing prayers for those about to go to war and possibly fighting as a soldier for the Northumbrian kings. Cuthbert lived through a period when attempts were made to reconcile differences in Roman and Celtic Church practices and calendars. Amongst the things that they disagreed about was the date of Easter. Although the Synod of Whitby in 664 declared for the Roman church and Cuthbert seemed to accept this, some of his practices suggest his spiritual heart remained with the Celtic tradition.

Mailros Abbey had neither the scale nor grandeur of David 1's later abbey nor its wealth and comforts. It was active as an abbey for a mere two centuries before it was destroyed in 859 on the orders of a dying Kenneth McAlpin. Over the 20 years of his rule as King of Dalriada and later Scotia, Kenneth had conducted a relentless campaign to push the Northumbrians back to the Cheviot Hills in a bid to unify Scotland. He was also keen to replace the Roman Church with the Celtic Church. If Mailros Abbey was gone, so were its monks and the links with Lindisfarne. However, as the abbey buildings melted into the landscape, the exceptional piety, not to say eccentricity of the denizens of Old Mailros lived on in the stories told by one generation to another.

Old Adam

During the more than 20 years Adam lived at Mailros he was never known to go in or out of bed. The straw that provided his mattress was never disturbed until eventually it would crumble to dust and, to avoid any kind of display, Adam would then request new straw for his bed which he laid on top of the old, as if he intended to sleep there.

Adam, however, had no need of a bed. He did sleep in snatches but in an upright posture at the altar of the Blessed Virgin, the Mother of God. There he spent the winter nights, playing on his harp and singing hymns to Our Lady. During the daytime he sat by the church door reciting the psalms in order, but always at his hand he kept a basket full of bread so that any poor person who came into the church could be fed.

He would often say that he was fortunate in having access to such provisions and that none should go away hungry or with any cause for complaint. Many people came to Mailros just to receive a blessing from Old Adam. In fact, many rich and powerful people, even the King, came to Adam anxious to give alms and entreat the good man's prayers for their souls. But Adam refused all gifts except for two cows which he milked so that he could offer the poor a drink of sweet milk with their bread.

Return to the A68, turn left and, at St Boswells, turn left onto B6404.

St Boswells was originally known by its Anglo-Saxon name of Lessudden but was later renamed for the Abbot of Mailros Abbey, Boisil, who, it is believed, set up a missionary outpost here.

The wide village green is what remains of an area of a common land and is where the St Boswells Fair is held annually. A much smaller affair now than it was, people travelled long distances to buy and sell livestock, goods and services at this most famous of fairs. Many came to party, engage in the sporting contests, or have their fortune told by a Yetholm gypsy.

The fair was famous for its horse trading, horses being the pride of the Borders. At one time as many as 1,000 horses might be traded over six days. It was a complex, lengthy and thirsty business. Buyers needed temporarily poor hearing and a good eye or as Andrew Scott, who lived in the late 18th and early 19th century in nearby Bowden, put it:

Here truth at times weel mix'd wi' lees
Defines their age or youth
While buyers trust to their ain ees
And cautious, look their mooth.

In addition to plentiful supplies of food and drink, there was entertainment. The revelling carried on well into the night, with adverse consequences for good order and health. For many, St Boswells Fair was the social highpoint of their year. James Hogg, the Ettrick Shepherd, shocked his patrons by turning down an invitation to King George IV's coronation because the date clashed with 'Bosils Fair'. No one in the Borders was surprised though – Hogg was renowned for his love of games and festivities, as well as his poems and tales.

Snowy white Lessudden House on the far edge of the village, and the tower it replaced, belonged to the Scotts of Raeburn – the branch from which Sir Walter Scott was descended. One of Walter's forebears became a Quaker at a time when being a member of any church other than the Presbyterian was to risk your life. None of the children became Quakers, but his heir took an equally risky path by becoming an ardent Jacobite. He vowed, after the last of three failed Jacobite risings, that he would not shave until there was a Stuart on the throne of Great Britain again. Subsequently nicknamed Beardie, he and his beard, which must by then have been impressive, are buried in Kelso Abbey.

Proceed through St Boswells, cross the Tweed and turn first right (signed Mertoun).

Set in the fine grounds and gardens of Mertoun House, built in the early 18th century where once there was a village, is Mertoun Kirk. This attractive wee church still has its 'jougs', where those who had contravened the strict 17th century moral codes were chained by the neck as punishment. Also surviving is the 'loupin' on stane', a set of stand-alone steps to make the business of getting onto or off a horse a more dignified business than it would, for women anyway, otherwise be.

This kirk replaced a much older 12th century one closer to the river which was founded around the same time as Dryburgh Abbey.

Old Mertoun House with its crow step gabling, now 'gardener's cottage', was built in the 18th century by Sir Walter Scott's relatives. Indeed, it was here as their guest that he wrote 'The Eve of St John', the first of many poems that made his name. In the introduction to Canto VI of Marmion he says of Mertoun at Christmas:

And Mertoun's halls are fair e'en now
When not a leaf is on the bough,
Tweed loves them well and turns again
As loath to leave the sweet domaine
And hold his mirror to her face
And clips her with a close embrace.

Of particular interest here, is the impressive beehive doocot built in 1567. It is the oldest surviving doocot of its kind thanks in part to a local superstition that if the laird were to destroy it, his wife would die within the year. No laird to date has put this to the test.

Return to B6404, turn left then immediately right onto B6356 (signed Dryburgh) and proceed to Dryburgh Abbey.

The road to Dryburgh delights with views up and down the Tweed valley before dropping down to Dryburgh and the picturesque ruins of its abbey. Founded in 1150 by Baron Hugh de Moreville Constable of Scotland and Lord of Lauderdale in another of the Tweed's horseshoe bends, the Abbey was later granted a charter of confirmation by David I. As at Melrose, there had been an earlier monastery here founded in the 6th century by St Modan. This was probably on or close to a site that had significance for the Celtic British who named the place Darach bruach – the mound of the oak trees.

And it is still a place of trees. Amongst the oldest trees in the grounds of Dryburgh Abbey are cedars said to date back to the 12th century and an

800-year-old yew tree. These trees have witnessed much in their time including English attacks on the Abbey in 1322, 1385 and a final attack in 1544. Amongst those buried here are Sir Walter Scott and Field Marshall Haig. They are not however amongst Dryburgh's ghosts, though plainsong has been heard coming from the Abbey buildings in the dead of night. And many have seen or heard the ghost of the Grey Lady as she stalks the Abbey and the nearby hotel. She is thought to have been the lover of a monk who, after he was murdered, drowned herself in the Tweed.

The monks of Dryburgh were Premonstratensians whose mission was to save souls by shriving people of their sins and saying mass daily. Over the 15th and early 16th centuries however, monks in this, and other abbeys, developed a reputation not only for breaking their vows of chastity but also of being overly concerned with making money for their already very wealthy institutions. A story that casts the monks of Dryburgh Abbey in that unfavourable light has long circulated in the area.

The Dryburgh Monks: A Tricky Tale

When the old laird of Meldrum was on his deathbed, he asked a visitor to go to the Abbey on the way home to tell the monks he was ready to confess his sins and be given the last rites. Two monks answered the call but found when they reached his house that they were too late. The laird had already departed this earth.

Old Meldrum had been a wealthy man and the monks, having prayed for his soul all these years, expected him to remember the Abbey in his will. They hunted high and low but there was no sign of anything resembling a will anywhere. Realising that no one else knew that Old Meldrum was already dead, the two monks hatched a plan – they would hide the body, bribe someone who looked like Old Meldrum to pretend to be him and summon a lawyer to come and write down Meldrum's last will and testament. And of course, Dryburgh Abbey would be the main beneficiary.

And so, Thomas Dickson, a local farmer who resembled Old Meldrum in build and looks, was summoned and persuaded to play the part of the dying man. The scene was quickly set up and a lawyer brought. Thomas Dickson sat up in bed and proceeded to give the lawyer his instructions. Pretty much everything was to be left, he said, to his good friend, honest Thomas Dickson. Well, the monks were speechless – and speechless they had to remain. They could hardly confess to the ruse now!

And so it was that Thomas Dickson came into a fortune and lived well thereafter. And the monks? From then on, their prayers regarding local farmers may have made up with ill-speaking what they lacked in charity.

This story reached a wider readership when it appeared in the 1830s in the Berwick Advertiser. It was one of many tales and ballads published as newspaper supplements by the editor John Mackay Wilson and his successors. So popular were these supplements that they were later collected and reprinted as *Wilson's Tales of the Borders* to become, for Borderers with money to spend, the coffee table books of their day.

Leaving the abbey, pass the entrance to Dryburgh Abbey Hotel and take minor road down to the Tweed.

This road leads to a pretty suspension footbridge across the Tweed to St Boswells and to the Temple of the Muses, a monument honouring James Thomson, the poet who wrote 'Rule Britannia'. His most inspiring poetic work is however 'The Seasons', which is credited with bringing a love of the natural world back into art and paving the way for the Romantic movement. An earlier monument on this site was commissioned by the eccentric 11th Earl of Buchan, a patriotic enthusiast for all things Scottish. He set about turning his Dryburgh estate into an early version of a theme park which also included the statue at our next stop.

Returning to the road turn left, left again at the top of the hill (signed Earlston) and, at the sign for Wallace Statue, left for optional walk.

A short woodland walk opens into a clearing in which stands a seven-metre-high statue of William Wallace. This larger than life statue commemorates a man with a giant reputation in Scottish history as the defender of Scottish Independence and indeed its chief martyr – after seven years on the run, he was captured and executed in 1305 on the order of Edward I. The statue, originally painted white, was erected in 1814. The Earl, an admirer of the French and American revolutions, had the statue positioned so that the unseeing Wallace looked across the Tweed towards the Cheviot Hills and across Ancrum Moor where, in 1545, the Scots defeated an English army. The significance of this victory was that it enabled Mary Queen of Scots to get to France to be married to the Dauphin of France and Scotland to remain an independent country. Had the English won, Mary would have been married to Henry VIII's son and Scotland would have become a dependency of England.

Exit car park to left and proceed to Bemersyde.

On your left as you reach Bemersyde village is the tower house and around it lands which have been in the hands of the Haig family since the mid-12th century. Thomas of Ercildoune, alias Thomas the Rhymer, witnessed a document here for Petrus de Haga. He also made the somewhat ambiguous prophecy that:

Betide, betide whate'er may betyde
Haig shall be Haig of Bemersyde

The family's extraordinarily long association with the land and house is due in part to good marriages and good luck but also to their ability to read the political situation and so avoid having their lands confiscated.

Proceed through Bemersyde and stop at Scott's View viewpoint.

This was, as the name of the place hints, one of Scott's favourite views. It was however his horses who staked their claim on it: accustomed to stopping here, they poignantly stopped unbidden in 1832 as they brought his body from Abbotsford to its final resting place at Dryburgh

Abbey. Laid out before us is a panoramic view of the places visited on this journey and a landscape that inspired George Ballantyne from Jedburgh to write:

> I stood above sweet Bemersyde, our fairest Border scene,
> And watched the undulation of the shadows with the green.
> I saw the river slowly bend, majestic in its flow,
> And heard – just like a whispering sigh – its torrent far below.
> I saw the lordly Eildons three, like giants frowning, stand,
> Their mist-clad summits seemed to breathe enchantment o'er the land.
> I gazed on field and forest green, parts of the mighty plan
> And in upon my soul was borne the thought how small is man.
> While abbeys crumble to decay, while mansions rise and fall
> While hamlets rise and disappear, and change is over all…
> Throughout all things, kind Nature moves, the earth with
>   sweetness fills
> While, massive still, as guardians stand the everlasting hills.

Continue on following signs for Leaderfoot, pass under the bridges and, at T junction beyond Gattonside, turn left across the Tweed and follow signs to Tweedbank Station.

Journey 2

Ettrick and Yarrow

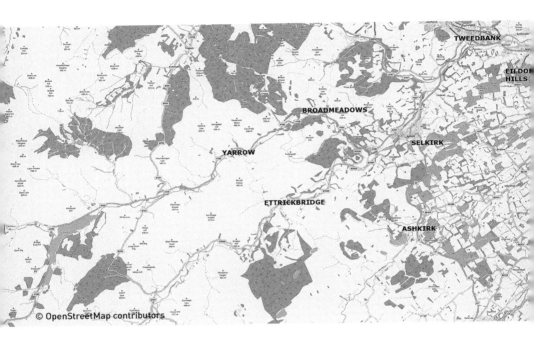

© OpenStreetMap contributors

This journey goes into the Ettrick and Yarrow valleys, a sparsely populated area with few villages and only one town, Selkirk. Rising in the southern uplands to the west, the Ettrick and Yarrow rivers are hemmed in and separated by hills, until the Yarrow joins the Ettrick and together they meet the Tweed near Abbotsford. Old drove roads down which black cattle were driven to southern markets wind across these hills as do sections of the Southern Upland Way, the National Cycle Route, the Walter Scott Way and the Buccleuch County Ride route.

The area was of little interest to the Romans or the Anglo Saxons. Getting to these remote valleys from the west, north or south involved a long trek and so there was little need for defences. The Scoto-Normans however saw them quite differently. These hills were economic and political gold to them. As part of David I's social, economic and legal reforms, he granted vast areas of land to his abbeys and to favoured nobles. The best hunting grounds however, he kept for himself. The Royal Ettrick Forest covered much of the Ettrick and Yarrow valleys and extended as far as Galashiels and Innerleithen. It was a favourite royal retreat and sporting playground for good reason:

> Ettrick Foreste is a fair foreste;
> In it grows many a semelie tree –
> There's hart and hind, and dae and rae.
> And of a' wilde bestis grete cragg.

Local place names like Hyndhope, Boarcleuch, Harewood echo these days. The tree clad hills also attracted outlaws, rebels and secret gatherings. In the early 14th century, a young freedom fighter William Wallace rallied men here in support of his bid to win back Scotland's independence from England.

Scotland did regain its independence but, for the next three centuries, the people of these two valleys were frequently caught up in English military efforts to win it back. Tower houses were built on royal order along all the main tributaries of the Tweed in the 15th and 16th centuries. With the exception of Selkirk's residents, the population of Ettrick and Yarrow were almost entirely dependent on the owners of tower houses for food, shelter and protection. Many of the most powerful Border families had bases in Ettrick or Yarrow – a safe distance from the border but close enough to get there quickly – and by the 15th century when they were not fighting against the English they were fighting and reiving each other.

In 1528 James V came up with a plan to tame the unruly Borderers and, at the same time, provide some sport. He invited Scotland's nobles to bring supplies for a month and to come hunting with him in Ettrick Forest. Twelve hundred nobles answered his call and, over several weeks, royal hunting parties killed around 360 deer and captured the 'heid men' of several Border families. Some were executed on the spot but most were locked up, tried, exiled or executed, and their lands confiscated. The king then had an additional 10,000 sheep put to graze in the forest to slow down woodland regeneration and make the area less attractive to outlaws, rebels and reivers. Even this and the 'slighting' (damaging) of towers just enough to make them undefendable did not 'daunton' the border reivers! Reiving persisted until the Union of the Crowns in 1603.

Life in the Ettrick and Yarrow valleys continued to be turbulent in the 17th century but for different reasons. What began as resistance to royal attempts to impose the beliefs and practices of the Episcopalian Church of England on Scotland's Presbyterian churchgoers after 1603, escalated by the middle of the century into a full blown civil war involving Scotland, Ireland and England.

A key bone of contention was the 'head of the church'. When Protestantism replaced Roman Catholicism during the previous century, the English church had recognised the monarch as its head. The Scots however chose a Calvinist version of Protestantism which tended towards democracy and, as a matter of principle, acknowledged no human head. The Covenanting movement attracted those who were not prepared to alter the way they worshipped. When Charles I insisted, the Covenanters gained control of the Scottish Parliament and the support of

English Parliamentarians, and took up arms. Charles I was eventually toppled and Great Britain had a taste of parliamentary rule before the Stuart kings regained the throne 11 years later in 1660. Charles II immediately revived the campaign to align the religious practice of Scottish and English churchgoers. He placed spies in communities and sent troops to root out dissenters. Covenanters were again outlaws. The more they were persecuted, the more extreme their views became and the stand-off continued. Many Ettrick and Yarrow men and women continued to worship at secret 'conventicles' in the hills despite the risk of the terrible consequences of being caught during what became known as 'the Killing Times' of the 1680s.

The Ettrick and Yarrow valleys are amongst the least populated areas of the eastern Borders. Trees and sheep tell few tales, but the landscape and its history conspired to touch imagination and emotion. T Ratcliffe Brown said of the Ettrick valley, 'a ballad meets you at every corner and in every grey old tower'. These sung stories relating the triumphs and disasters befalling members of mostly prominent families are almost as thick on the ground in the Yarrow valley. Like many tales passing through many lips, historical accuracy is variable. Many however retain the pre-Christian reverence for nature and its bounty, a reverence which revived in the writings of the Romantics in the 18th and 19th centuries. The stories and songs also retain the belief in omens, spirits and magic and, as Sir Walter Scott, whose maternal and paternal family roots were here, noted, 'In no part of Scotland, indeed, has the belief in Fairies maintained its ground with more pertinacity than in Selkirkshire'.

As we journey up the Ettrick and back down the Yarrow valley, we get a sense of why these landscapes inspired travellers and residents alike to put pen to paper, why the Ettrick ballads are dominated by stories of daring raids and rescues, honour killings and arranged marriages; and why the Yarrow ballads offer melancholy tales of loss reflecting the human cost of family feuds, and tragic ends to inconvenient love matches.

Along the way, we meet the Souters of Selkirk, witches and wizards, a young man poisoned by his wicked stepmother, a self-educated shepherd poet and novelist, Nudus and Domogenes sons of Liberalis, and some Covenanters. We also hear a lot about a family named Scott.

The Journey: 84 miles

Part One: Ettrick

From Tweedbank Station follow signs for A7 (signed Galashiels), cross the Tweed and take first exit at roundabout onto A7 south (signed Selkirk/Carlisle). Proceed to Selkirk town centre and park.

The hillside town of Selkirk grew up around a 12th century castle which, like the native British Iron Age site beneath it, overlooked the Ettrick between its junction with the Yarrow upstream and the Tweed downstream. David I founded the castle and also an abbey here, but relocated the abbey to Kelso later in the century and the castle was abandoned in the early 14th century after one too many batterings by the English trying to oust the Scots or vice versa.

Thanks to the grant of Royal Burgh status, though, the town survived. Selkirk's merchants imported goods from abroad and craftsmen supplied local and international buyers with cloth, shoes and boots made from local wool and cattle hides. Selkirk's fame as a shoemaking town gave those born there the name of 'souters'. The shoemaking industry fell victim to mass production techniques long ago, but the 'souter' tag remains.

The town was also an important producer of woollen textiles and, having survived the three-century journey from hand produced to the ironically termed digitised production methods, it still is! Cloth was initially made of hand-spun yarn by handloom weavers in and around the town. Then from the 1820s, thanks to Selkirk's location on the Ettrick which had a flow strong enough to power machinery, large quantities of quality cloth rolled off the new-fangled mechanised looms and into far flung markets. The mills which survived the 20th century crisis in the industry continue to supply cloth to world markets.

Some of the many renowned characters who figure in Selkirk's story do so literally. This small town has a lot of statues! There is one of Mungo Park, a 19th century doctor and African explorer born at nearby Foulshiels, who died aged only 34 attempting to find the source of the river Niger. And another is of Sir Walter Scott outside the courtroom where he carried out the duties of his day job as 'the shirra' (Sheriff) of Selkirkshire. And, until the gate post it was fixed to was knocked down, there was a plaque commemorating Andrew Lang, another Selkirk Souter. Born in 1844, Lang was an eminent historian, anthropologist and a prolific writer, novelist and poet. His immersion in the stories and tales of the Borders and, in particular, the Ettrick and Yarrow valleys sparked a lifelong passion for folklore and fascination with the fairy folk. He published 12 volumes of fairy stories collected from around the world, to each of which he allocated not a number but a colour.

The most poignant of Selkirk's statues however is that of John Fletcher. Said to be the sole Selkirk resident to return from Flodden in 1513, he staggered into the market square with a tattered English flag which he found the strength to wave around his head before throwing it down to signal that all was lost. This event is commemorated annually at Selkirk Common Riding when the Standard Bearer, who in the past would have been selected from one of the town's medieval craft guilds, re-enacts Fletcher's flag casting.

We return to Selkirk towards the end of this journey but before we leave, a ghostly tale of what happened when one of Selkirk's souters accepted an unusual commission to make a pair of shoes.

Shoes for a Dead Man

The Souters of Selkirk began work before dawn to make sure they had finished shoes ready for order or immediate sale. One morning a shoemaker in Kirk

Wynd was visited by a stranger who ordered a pair of shoes to be ready in a few days at a specific time.

On the agreed day and time, the stranger collected his shoes. The Souter though felt there was something strange in the man's dress and his manner, so he followed his erstwhile customer along Kirk Wynd and into the kirkyard. Imagine his shock when the stranger vanished into a recently dug grave!

The Souter, who still had his awl in his hand, stuck it into the turf beside this grave and went to summon help. Soon he had a gaggle of cronies, acquaintances and hangers on, all agog at the shaken man's account. They duly dug up the grave, prised open the coffin, and found the newly made shoes inside. A frisson of delighted horror ran round the crowd. Although he had been paid fair and square for the footwear in question, the Souter retrieved the shoes and took them back to his shop.

Early the next morning, the Souter was at his workbench when, lo and behold, the stranger appeared before him, his face a mask of fury. Accusing the shoemaker of stealing his fairly purchased shoes, he then said, 'You have made a mockery of me – but I will make you a world's wonder.'

Without further ado, the fearsome visitant seized the Souter with more than natural strength, and dragged him to the kirkyard. There his body was found, later that day, mangled and bloodied. No culprit was ever found or punished. The broken body of the poor Souter was swiftly gathered up and buried in the same graveyard. But, in contrast to the crowd that had attended the digging up the day before, there was a scant hantle of folk at the shoemaker's burying.

Exit Selkirk on A707, turn left at junction with B7009 (signed Ettrickbridge), right onto B7039 (signed Yarrow Valley) and stop at Tamlane's Well.

Crossing the Ettrick to the low land lying between the Yarrow and Ettrick rivers just before they merge, takes us onto Carterhaugh. Archaeological finds attest to this river junction's importance as an ancient gathering place for the Celtic British and probably others before them. This was later a site for traditional ball games. In one famous contest the men of Selkirk took on the shepherds of Ettrick and Yarrow – an idea hatched over a 19th century dinner party at nearby Bowhill. By the time the match date came around the numbers of both teams had grown dramatically. Not only had people travelled from far and wide to join one team or other but many, including Walter Scott and James Hogg, came just to watch. Such games may be the origin of a local song, sometimes erroneously ascribed to Flodden:

Up wi' the Souters o Selkirk
And doun wi' the Earl of Home!
And up wi' the braw lads
That sew the single-soled shoon.
Fie upon yellow and yellow,
and fie upon yellow and green,
But up wi' the true blue and scarlet,
And up wi' the single-soled shoon.
Up wi' the Souters o Selkirk,
For they are baith trusty and leal;
And up wi' the men o the Forest,
And doun wi' the Merse to the Deil.

Carterhaugh was also believed to be a place where the boundary between the fairy and human worlds was flimsy, and particularly so at turning points in the year. Tamlane's Well marks the place where young Tam Lin or Tamlane was dramatically rescued from his fairy captors by his young lover Janet one Halloween lang syne.

Tamlane

Janet, daughter perhaps of the Earl of March, ignored the strict advice to all young women *'That wear gowd in your hair'*, to stay out of the forest of Carterhaugh lest they meet Tamlane for,

There's nane that gaes by Carterhaugh
But they leave him a wad,

> *Either their rings, or green mantles,*
> *Or else their maidenhead.*

Such are the perils of 'fairy magic'. Wandering in the forest one day Janet comes to a well. She stops to pick one of the roses growing there when, from its petals emerges a handsome young man. He asks why she is in Carterhaugh pulling roses without his permission. She replies that this is her father's land and she doesn't need his permission. After that frosty exchange, Janet learns that Tamlane is in fact a nobleman entrapped by the Queen of Fairy, and the mood thaws.

A few months later it becomes obvious that Janet is pregnant. She declines offers of marriage from elderly suitors concerned to protect her reputation but no doubt also keen to get the dowry she would bring, and runs off to Carterhaugh saying,

> *'If that I gae wi' child, father,*
> *Mysel' maun bear the blame,*
> *There's ne'er a laird about your ha',*
> *Shall get the bairn's name'.*

Once again, she picks a rose hoping to summon Tamlane and once again he appears. He tells her that his fairy captors plan to hand him over to the devil to settle their seven-yearly obligation to surrender one human soul that very night – Halloween – and that the only way to escape that fate is for his true love to pull him from his horse at midnight as he passes with the fairy queen and her entourage. But, he warns her, the queen will do all she can to make her let go of him. Janet though is not easily put off and resolves to dare the worst.

> *Gloomy, gloomy was the nicht,*
> *And eery was the way,*
> *As fair Janet in her green mantle*
> *To Milescross she did gae.*
> *About the deid hoor o' the nicht*
> *She heard the bridles ring,*
> *And Janet was as glad o' that*
> *As ony earthly thing.*

As Tamlane passes in the fairy procession, Janet pulls him off his horse. But the handsome Tamlane turns into an eel – she holds on – then he turns into an adder – she holds on – then a bear and then a lion. With each change, she holds on tight. Finally, the fairy queen turns him into a red-hot ember. Somehow, Janet grasps it tight and, remembering what he had told her to do, she runs to this very well and throws in the ember. When Tamlane steps naked from the well, Janet throws her green mantle over him to hide him until the fairy troop ride on. Their Queen was enraged by the loss of 'the bonniest knight o all her companie'.

> 'If I had known, Tamlane,' she says,
> What I this nicht hae seen,
> Ah wud hae pit out your twa grey een,
> An' pit in twa een o tree.'

Tamlane, having escaped the fate the fairies intended, is free to marry Janet. Not so much a lucky escape as a determined rescue driven by love and also perhaps by Janet's determination to claim her child's father.

Returning to B7009 junction turn right (signed Ettrickbridge).

Rounding the long bend after Carterhaugh, we glimpse above the trees on the left a magnificently restored 16th century tower house. Aikwood or Oakwood Tower, now in private hands, was built by ancestors of Sir Walter Scott on or near the site of an older tower which was said to have been home to Michael Scot, the 13th century wizard. He spent most of his time in Europe but one wizardly episode took place close to home and involved an alleged witch at nearby Fauldshope.

The Witch of Fauldshope

One day Michael Scott decided to pay a visit to the wife of the farmer at Fauldshope to find out if there was any truth in the rumours that she was a witch – and a mean one at that.

When he got to their cottage, as was usual in these parts, he shouted a greeting and went in. But the farmer's wife was not at all pleased to see him. 'I am far too busy to have you in for a blether. Away you go!' she snapped. And before Michael could stop her, she grabbed his stick, tapped him on the shoulder with it and mumbled something. Instantly, Michael felt himself shrinking. Then his ears started to grow. And now he was growing fur! Soon he was covered in the stuff and instead of two legs he had four. The wicked woman had turned him into a hare with his very own stick! So, she *was* a witch.

Michael's first thought was that he had to get back to Aikwood to consult his Book of Magic on how to undo the spell. So he started running. And his dogs, who didn't know the hare was Michael, chased after him. It was a close-run thing but Michael got back to Aikwood before the dogs, wriggled into the house through a drain, and did what he had to do to break the witch's spell.

Michael was, understandably, furious. Now, he knew that the witch took freshly baked bread to the fields every day at this time of year to feed the people working there with her husband. And so, a few days later Michael sent one of his men to ask if she could spare some bread. True to form, the mean old besom claimed she had no bread to spare. Michael had anticipated this and had given his man a piece of paper to slip onto the lintel above the door to the cottage. The paper said – *Maister Scot's man asked for bread and got nane.*

No sooner had Michael's man done this when the witch was seized by the urge to dance. It was time to take the lunch to the workers in the fields but she just had to dance. And once she started she couldn't stop. On and on she danced. After a while, her husband sent a boy to find out where the lunch had got to. But when the boy ran into the house he too was seized by an irresistible urge to dance. Round and round he danced with the witch.

When the boy didn't come back, the farmer assumed he had got lost or distracted and sent an older boy. When he didn't come back either, the farmer set off to the cottage himself. Imagine his surprise when he passed the kitchen window and saw his wife and the two boys dancing around the kitchen, gasping for breath like fish out of water, with faces as red as a robin redbreast's chest.

He guessed right away of course who might be responsible and ran off to Aikwood Tower. When he got there, Michael owned up, told him why he had put a spell on his wife and how to break it. The farmer followed Michael's instructions when he got home and right away the dancing stopped. Of course, his wife and the two boys were in no fit state to take the lunch out to the workers so the farmer had to take it himself. As far as we know the farmer's wife never danced again. And, if she had any sense, never again did she refuse to share her time or her food.

Many years later, a woman who lived up the valley at Deloraine was outed as a witch when a thirsty apprentice unwittingly revealed the secret of the plentiful supply of milk workmen enjoyed at her house. He had watched the woman fill a jug from a tap in the wall and, when nobody was looking, went to help himself. But, to his horror, when he had drunk his fill he found he could not turn the tap off. The milk carried on flowing until the sight of a river of milk flowing past her cottage door brought the woman running to turn the tap off. Sadly for her and her visitors, that was the end of milk on tap in Ettrick. When the story got about it confirmed her neighbours' suspicions – she had been using magic to milk the cows of her neighbours as well as her own. There was little harm in 'borrowing' a little milk now and again, you might think. However, by the time the tap was turned off, cows the length and breadth of the Ettrick valley had been milked and there was not a drop of milk to be had until the next milking time.

The witches of Fauldshope and Deloraine got off lightly compared with those who were accused by their neighbours of being witches in the 17th century. They suffered terrifying ordeals and indignities in the name of establishing their guilt or innocence and, either way, met their ends by drowning or burning.

As we travel from Fauldshope to Deloraine, we go through Ettrickbridge where the river channel squeezes through the narrow Kirkhope Linns. Stories involving water spirits are rare in the Tweed catchment area and ones involving mischievous rather than malicious spirits are even rarer. But it was here, so the story goes, that a mischievous bogle led two passing travellers a merry dance.

The Bogle

Not long after two men had set off towards their next destination, they heard cries of 'Lost! Lost!' coming from the river. Thinking someone was in dire trouble they followed the cries which were repeated but never seemed to get any closer. Several hours later, after following the elusive voice further and further up the valley, the men came to the source of the river. They were still hearing cries of 'Lost! Lost!', taking them up a hill. As they neared the top they could still hear the cries but now they were coming from the other side of the hill.

Exhausted and miles away from their intended destination, they gave up the quest and turned back. And then, as they later told people, they heard hoots and howls of laughter coming from the other side of the hill and knew they had been tricked by a bogle. Perhaps drink was involved in the two travellers' wanderings but some kind of bogle did lead them a merry dance.

Tucked away in the hills above Ettrickbridge is Kirkhope Tower, once a stronghold of this branch of the Scott family. Auld Wat of Harden as he became known throughout the Borders was one of the most hardened and feared of the Borders reivers. Such was his reputation that when James VI ordered the demolition of this defiant chief's many towers, none were brave enough to carry out his bidding. Kirkhope Tower was for a time the home of Wat Scott and his wife Mary, the Flower of Yarrow, of whom more shortly.

Travelling on, we pass in quick succession the site of Hyndhope Tower on the left and, on the right, the site of Gilmanscleuch Tower. This was owned by yet another branch the Scott family. Members of the extended Scott family were frequently at loggerheads with one another and there are many fatal tales. One particular Scott death was avenged in an unusual way that showed up Auld Wat of Harden, the father of the dead lad, as heartless but clever.

Wily Auld Wat

One of Wat and Mary's six sons was killed by the Gilmanscleuch Scotts at a hunt which got out of hand. His remaining five sons were baying for revenge but Auld Wat was a wily man. He shut his vengeful sons up in the Kirkhope Tower dungeon and rode post-haste to Edinburgh, to appeal to the King for restitution. Surely, he argued, he should be compensated for the loss of a son with the lands of the lad's killers. The King agreed. Auld Wat on the side of due process for once!

Returning to Kirkhope, he released his sons from the dungeon and showed them the charter for the lands of Gilmanscleuch he had secured from a bemused King. 'Tae horse, laddies,' he is said to have cried as he set off to claim his compensation, 'the lands of Gilmanscleuch are weill worth a deid son!'

Auld Wat's raiding ways were notorious on both sides of the border between Scotland and England with booty sometimes numbering three or four hundred head of cattle. If it moved it was fair game as far as Wat was concerned! Passing a large haystack on the way home from a raid, he is alleged to have looked at it with longing and said 'Gin ye had fower feet ye wouldna bide there lang.'

Pass Crosslee and at the Y junction take the left fork onto B709 (signed Langholm).

Just beyond the junction we pass what little remains of Tushielaw Tower on the right. There are many stories associated with this tower and the branch of the Scott family who lived here. Most involve battles but this one, related in verse by James Hogg, in the Queen's Wake, has a rare happy ending.

The Sleeping Beauty of Ettrick

Mary Scott, the daughter of the Scotts of Tushielaw (not be confused with Mary Scott, Flower of Yarrow mentioned above) had her heart set on marrying Pringle of Torwoodlee over on Gala Water. And so smitten was he by her that he disguised himself as a priest in order to get time alone with her. There was however no love lost between the two families, and Mary's father was vehemently opposed to the notion of having a Pringle as son-in-law.

Mary's mother however could not bear to see her daughter so sad and hatched a plan. She gave Mary a drink laced with a sleeping potion which took her to the brink of death. So deathlike was she that everyone but her mother believed she had died. Dressed by her mother in the finest clothes, her coffin was taken to St Mary's Kirk at the top of Yarrow to be buried.

In those days, coffins were left open so that family, friends and neighbours could say their farewells. At the very moment a sad Pringle of Torwoodlee approached the coffin and bent to kiss her brow, she opened her eyes. She was alive! There was great rejoicing and her father agreed, albeit grudgingly, to the marriage. We know he was still unhappy about the match because he paid Mary's dowry in cattle, which it later came to light he had stolen, or in the parlance of the day, 'reived' or 'lifted'.

This tale, as told by James Hogg the Ettrick Shepherd, draws on unrivalled local knowledge. But his story is a reworking of the anonymous Yarrow ballad 'The Gay Goss Hawk'. In this, the messenger between a Sir William and his highborn lover is the lord's favourite hawk, which brings to him under its 'grey pinion' a letter. In it she promises to come to St Mary's Kirk and lie there for Sir William as if dead. Here, a cruel stepmother is the barrier between the lovers, but she is thwarted by the instructions the daughter leaves when she 'dies'.

> *The first Scots kirk that they cam to,*
> *They garred the bells be rung;*
> *The next Scots kirk that they cam to,*
> *They garred the Mass be sung.*
> *But when they cam to St Mary's Kirk,*
> *There stude spearmen all on a row;*
> *And up started Lord William,*
> *The chieftain amang them aa.*
> *'Set down, set down the bier,' he said,*
> *'Let me look her upon';*
> *But as soon as Lord William touched her hand,*
> *Her colour began to come.*
> *She brightened like the lily flower,*

Till her pale hue was gone;
With rosy cheek and ruby lip,
She smiled her love upon.
'A morsel of your bread, my lord,
And one glass of your wine;
For I have fasted these three lang days,
All for your sake and mine.'

Between Tushielaw and Ettrick the river meanders past the sites of three more tower houses. Thirlestane was held for a time by yet another branch of the Scott family and Gamescleuch was originally built for Simon, son of John Scott of Thirlestane as a wedding present from his father. Sadly, the couple never got to live in the house because, on the evening of their marriage, Simon unexpectedly died. It was rumoured that this fit young man was poisoned by his stepmother who, determined to ensure that her children inherited her husband's wealth and land, was prepared to commit murder. The last of these abandoned towers is Ramseycleuch.

At Y junction on B709 take right fork onto minor road with passing places (signed Ettrick).

Arriving in Ettrick Village we are in the heart of James Hogg the Ettrick Shepherd's world. Ettrick was at one time a large village but, by Hogg's time, it had shrunk considerably. An 18th century Laird of Tushielaw terminated the leases of tenants with small amounts of land to create larger farms which, with new farming methods, were more productive. Without alternative employment, many left Ettrick and other parts of the Scottish Borders in what later became known as the Lowland Clearances.

James Hogg, whose poetry and novels are more read than ever, not only witnessed these changes but grew up immersed in this landscape and the history of the area. He was inspired by the writings of Robert Burns, encouraged and influenced by Walter Scott, but influenced above all by his mother Margaret Laidlaw. From her he heard stories and ballads of local family feuds, bravery, ill-fated lovers and tragic romances in the near and distant past, and of witchcraft and the fairy folk. In his own day, Hogg was hailed by the literary world as 'King of the Mountain and the Fairy School'.

Indeed, James Hogg claimed to be descended from the Witch of Fauldshope, the very witch who allegedly turned Michael Scot into a hare. His grandfather, Will o' Phaup was reputed to be the last man in the Scottish Borders to talk to the fairies. Hogg's mother Margaret inherited his stock of stories and was persuaded to tell some of them to her son's new friend Walter Scott. He included some of them in his bestseller, 'The Minstrelsy of the Scottish Borders'. Margaret and her father lived at the end of an era and in a place where older beliefs and Christianity had a place in popular culture. Margaret did not however approve of her songs being written down. As she told Walter Scott, 'There niver was ane o' ma sangs prentit until ye prentit them yourself and you hae spoilt them aathegither. They were made for singing and no for readin and they'll never be sung nae mair'. Happily, she was wrong about that!

James Hogg, his parents and grandparents are amongst those buried in the graveyard of Ettrick Kirk. Hogg's birthplace, Ettrickhall Farm, is long gone but a monument marks the spot and the old school hosts a James Hogg exhibition in the summer months. These lines from Hogg's 'The Queen's Wake' sum up his deep attachment to this place:

> O, Ettrick! Shelter of my youth!
> Thou sweetest glen of all the south!
> Thy fairy tales and songs of yore,
> Shall never find my bosom more.
> Thy winding glades, and mountains wild,
> The scenes that pleased me when a child,
> Each verdant vale and flowery lea,
> Still in my midnight dreams I see;
> And waking oft, I sigh for thee.

Equally poignant is Lady John Scott's poem, 'Ettrick', recalling the emotions evoked riding down the valley at three points in her life. Also known by her maiden name, Alicia Jane Spottiswode, Lady Scott's motto *Haud fast tae the past* reflected her keen interest in the folk tales and traditions of the Borders. Her poem though is personal and poignant:

> *When we first rade down Ettrick,*
> *Our bridles were ringing, our hearts were dancing,*
> *The waters were singing, the sun was glancing,*
> *An' blithely our hearts rang out thegither,*
> *As we brushed the dew frae the blooming heather,*
> *When we first rade down Ettrick.*
>
> *When we next rade down Ettrick,*
> *The day was dying, the wild birds calling,*
> *The wind was sighing, the leaves were falling,*
> *An' silent an' weary, but closer thegither,*
> *We urged our steeds thro' the faded heather,*
> *When we next rade down Ettrick.*
>
> *When I last rade down Ettrick,*
> *The winds were shifting, the storm was waking,*
> *The snow was drifting, my heart was breaking,*
> *For we never again were to ride thegither,*
> *In sun or storm on the mountain heather,*
> *When I last rade down Ettrick.*

In Hogg's day, Ettrick Kirk and the lonely glens beyond were best known as the refuge of the 17th century Covenanters who maintained their stern faith here in defiance of the authorities. In 1707 Thomas Boston came to be Ettrick's minister, upholding the Puritan tradition but with a new glow of evangelical warmth, and an open door to faith in opposition to Calvinist predestination. After early struggles, Boston came to be much loved and people came from all over the Borders to hear him preach, latterly, in his illness, from a bedroom window. 'Give me the Bible and Boston, and you can take away every other book', was a later saying among Scotland's pious Presbyterians. There is an impressive memorial to Thomas Boston in the kirkyard.

The road beyond Ettrick continues to the source of the river but is a dead end so here we turn around to head back the way we came.

Return to the A709 (signed Selkirk).

A road to our right just before Tushielaw leads to wild Buccleuch, once a separate parish and home to the branch of the Scott family who were to become much later Dukes of Buccleuch. Legend has it that Kenneth McAlpin, first King of Scots, was hunting in Ettrick when he pursued a buck up the Rankleburn to Buccleuch where it stood at bay in a deep ravine. One John of Galloway climbed down and, taking the beast by the horns, dragged it to the King for the kill. He was immediately granted the lands and re-named Scott of Buck-cleuch. An unlikely history perhaps but a good tale which Walter Scott was happy to retell:

> Old Buccleugh the name did gain
> When in the cleuch the buck was ta'en.

At junction beyond Tushielaw swing left to continue on B709 (signed Innerleithen) and proceed to Gordon Arms Hotel junction.

Part Two: Yarrow and St Mary's Loch

Cutting through the hills to the Yarrow valley on the evocatively named Berrybush Road, we pass Hartleap where, in 1530 a hart fleeing royal hunters took a death defying nine metre leap across a deep cleft in the hillside. Then passing Altrieve, the farm James Hogg had rent free in later life from the Duke of Buccleuch (his dying wife asked him to remember 'the poor poet'), we enter the Yarrow valley at what was once an important junction. At our back is the Ettrick Valley; ahead of us the upper reaches of the Tweed; to our left St Mary's Loch and routes through the hills to Tweedsmuir and Dumfries and Galloway; and to the right, Selkirk and the middle and lower Tweed. And presiding over the comings and goings is the Gordon Arms, a gathering place for locals, and a stopping off point for travellers.

Behind the Gordon Arms is Mountbenger, the view from which so evoked the spirit of the Yarrow for James Hogg that from a vantage point on its slopes, he wrote 'By a bush':

Oft on thee the silent wain
Saw the Douglas banners streaming;
Oft on thee the hunter train
Sought the shelter'd deer in vain;
Oft in thy green dells and bowers,
Swains have seen the fairies riding.
Oft the snell and wintry showers
Found in thee the warrior hiding.
Many a wild and bloody scene
On thy bonny banks have been.

In his classic study of the poetry and history of the Borders, John Veitch describes Yarrow as 'a rough and broken, yet clear, beautiful and wide spreading stream' with a changeable quality that makes the scenery 'suitable for the nurture and expression of varying emotion – the notes of joy and grief'. Certainly, several poems inspired by the river begin joyfully enough but then relate a tale of woe. As JB Selkirk wrote in his 'Song of Yarrow':

It was not joy, it was not sorrow
A strange heart-fulness of them both
The wandering singer seemed to borrow
Like one that sings and does not know,
But in a dream hears voices calling
Of those who died long years ago.

65

This stretch of the river certainly witnessed some sad moments. At the Murder Moss a jilted older lover, pretending to accept a young woman's decision to go off with a younger suitor, offered to lead her and her new lover to the safety of the road, but led them instead into a marsh and to their deaths.

As Andrew Lang wrote of Yarrow 'its charm affects each one differently, each must see and feel for himself... whether the season be sweetest summertide or that when winters blast come black and raging down the glens.'

At Gordon Arms junction turn left onto A708 (signed St Mary's Loch).

As the Yarrow flows out of St Mary's Loch through a wide treeless valley it appears to be floating. Gold washed down from the surrounding hills was once found here in large enough quantities to cause a mini gold rush. The creation of reservoirs beyond St Mary's Loch later put paid to that, leaving the river banks to local birdlife.

High in the hills to the right above Craig Douglas is what little remains of Blackhouse Tower. There had been a house there since the 11th century, but in the late 18th century it was occupied by the Laidlaw family. They employed James Hogg as a shepherd for what were possibly the most important ten years of his life since, knowing of his interest in books, the Laidlaws gave him free access to their library. Here too he met Sir Walter Scott for the first time.

Earlier in its long life, Blackhouse Tower belonged to the Douglas family as did a castle at nearby Craig Douglas. The family played a prominent part in Scotland's mediaeval struggle to remain an independent nation. William Douglas fought with Wallace and later paid for his loyalty with his life. His son James fought with Robert the Bruce at Bannockburn, and became known to Scots as the Good James Douglas and to the English as the Black Douglas. His descendants went on to build further on their fame and political success. They were seen by the 15th century,

Newark Tower

with justification, as a threat to the monarch and publicly toppled – literally and metaphorically. In 1440, two young Douglas brothers were invited by the ten-year-old James II to Edinburgh Castle to attend what became known as the 'Black Dinner'. In a scene as gory as any horror film, a boar's head was delivered to the table signalling to all present that the young king, egged on by his advisers, had another agenda. Things did not end well for the two young guests: they were seized and beheaded. Twelve years later, King James II, still concerned that the Douglases were plotting to depose him, stabbed and killed the 8th Earl and, to prevent the family rallying support for their cause, stripped them of their lands and properties, including Blackhouse and Newark Castle further down the Yarrow valley. There was no coming back from that!

Sometime before their fall from grace, when they were still resident at Blackhouse, a tragedy befell the Douglas family which became the subject of a ballad, one of many telling of the fatal consequences of forbidden love. The ballad goes by two names: The Blackhouse Tragedy and The Douglas Tragedy.

The Blackhouse Tragedy

Margaret, a daughter of the Black Douglas, had become very fond of young Will Scott from Tweeddale and had decided he was the one for her. But no amount of pleading with her father could persuade him that she should be allowed to marry him. Will Scott's family was of lower social rank and an unsuitable match for the daughter of the mighty Douglas. Having pronounced on the matter, Douglas no doubt thought that was an end of it. Margaret and Will however had different ideas. One moonlight night, she sneaked out and off they rode towards Tweeddale.

Margaret's mother, who had been keeping a close eye, realised pretty quickly she was gone. She woke the household and urged the men to chase after the lovers. Her daughter's reputation and family honour was at stake!

> 'Rise up, rise up, now, Lord Douglas,' she says,
> 'And put on your armour so bright;
> Let it never be said that a daughter of thine
> Was married to a lord under night.
>
> 'Rise up, rise up, my seven bold sons,
> And put on your armour so bright.
> And take better care of your youngest sister,
> For your eldest's awa' the last night.'

So Margaret's seven brothers and her father saddled up and went in pursuit of the fleeing lovers. They followed a bridle path over the hills which was used to move animals and fighting men between the towers. The pursuers soon caught up with the fleeing couple, leaving Will no option but to turn and fight.

As is the chivalrous way, he took on each man in turn, killed all seven of Margaret's brothers and wounded her father. Torn between loyalty to her father and to her lover, Margaret chose Will. There was, after all, no way back for her. They rode on and stopped to drink from a stream, but Margaret suspected that Will too was injured:

> 'Hold up, hold up, Lord William,' she said,
> For I fear that you are slain'.

To which he replied:

> *'Tis naething but the shadow of my scarlet cloak,*
> *That shines in the water sae plain'.*

On they rode and when they arrived at Will's humbler tower house his mother took them in and made up a bed for them. Will was indeed mortally wounded and was dead before midnight. Margaret, too, was dead by morning. The ballad leaves us to guess how she died but, whatever the cause, both were buried at St Mary's Kirk of Yarrow.

> *Out o' the lady's grave grew a bonny red rose*
> *And out o' the knight's a brier.*
> *And they twa met, and they twa plat.*
> *And fain they wad be near;*
> *And a' the warld might ken right weel,*
> *They were twa lovers dear.*
> *But bye and rade the Black Douglas,*
> *And wow but he was rough!*
> *For he pull'd up the bonny brier,*
> *And flang'd in St Marie's Loch.*

Local lore has it that seven stones mark the spot on hillside where Margaret's seven brothers were slain. It is a touching story but there are in fact 11 stones, the remains of a larger group of standing stones put there around three millennia earlier.

This story is one of many tales of families going to extreme lengths to prevent their feistier daughters marrying or running away with lads considered unsuitable matches. Children, particularly daughters, were valuable resources and squandering your assets on marriages with no social or economic benefit was bad housekeeping. Curiously, few ballads tell of desperate measures being taken to prevent oldest sons making unwise matches!

Travelling on to where the road meets St Mary's Loch, Dryhope Tower sits up on the right. Dick of Dryhope was amongst those who in 1596 mounted a daring rescue from Carlisle Castle of Kinmont Willie. Dryhope Tower is however best known for being the home of the beautiful Mary Scott, Flower of Yarrow, who married the renowned border reiver Wat Scot of Kirkhope in the Ettrick valley. They were cousins and, in what was undoubtedly a dynastic but successful union, their marriage brought together two branches of the Scotts.

Besides feuding with opposing factions within the family and with families on both sides of the border, Wat Scott conspired with an illegitimate son of James v, Francis Stewart Earl of Bothwell, to seize the king. The plan failed and the king, no longer able to trust Wat Scott, ordered that Dryhope where Wat and Mary were living at the time be 'slighted'. To add insult to injury, he instructed Watt Scott's arch enemy, an equally ruthless Armstrong who later himself fell foul of the king, to carry out this order.

Progressing along the side of the loch, where the road takes a bend to the left, a blue sign points uphill to St Mary's Kirkyard. It is a fairly steep brae up to the kirkyard where the lovers of the Blackhouse Tragedy are buried but the views over the loch are magnificent. There was a church, St Mary's of the Lowes or the 'Kirk in the Forest', here too at one time. This was where Scotland's nobles assembled in 1297 to proclaim William Wallace Guardian of Scotland. And an annual 'blanket preaching' takes place here to commemorate the Covenanters who gathered in secret to worship and sat on blankets or, if it was raining, draped them over their heads. Watch Law, overlooking the graveyard, is a reminder that during the Killing Times of the 1680s it was necessary to post a watchman during services.

On the opposite side of the loch is Bowerhope or Bourhope about which Walter Elliot, the Borders scholar, poet, and tradition bearer, tells a story that provides some relief from the religious struggles of yesteryear. One sunny day the Bourhope folk went home from a 'hellfire and damnation' sermon at the Kirk and sat down to their dinner. Dinner was forgotten though when they noticed that on the other side of the loch each gravestone was arrayed in shining white. They fell to their knees in terror thinking that the Last Judgement had come and the dead were rising from their tombs. In fact, Jock the pedlar, having sat too long at Tibbie Shiel's Inn, had tipped his whole pack of white linen into a ditch. Consequently, he had laid it all out to dry on the gravestones in the kirkyard. Finally, in the absence of trumpets sounding, someone opened their eyes to see the dry linen waving in the wind.

We visit Tibbie Shiel's Inn shortly but first a short detour to the site of another evocative legend.

At Cappercleuch junction turn right onto minor road with passing places (signed Tweedsmuir).

This interesting road leads over to the Meggat and Talla Reservoirs and Tweedsmuir. We however go a mile and a half or so up it to where, on the right, are the ruins of Henderland Tower and, a little further on, 'Cockburn's Tomb' set on a wooded mound above the lovely stream that flows from the Dhu Linn or waterfall. This place has the feel of an early Celtic religious site although all that remains above ground is one medieval carved stone. But this peaceful spot is associated both with bloody past events and with the poetry of loss.

William Cockburn, the 16th century owner of Henderland Tower had a reputation for terrorising his neighbours. He and Adam Scott of Tushielaw over on Ettrick, known as the 'King of Thieves', were notorious for demanding 'black mail' – protection money or goods. The young James V was therefore especially keen to catch and make an example of them. And in 1529 he did just that. Both Cockburn and Scott were taken captive and dragged off to Edinburgh where, to drive home the message that no one was above the law, they were both duly tried then executed. The Cockburn in the grave below the Linn is not therefore this ruthless reiver but another of the same name. The facts of

Cockburn's death notwithstanding, word went around that Cockburn had been hung in his own front door and that Cockburn's wife had run to hide behind the Dhu Linn to drown out his screams. Her story then became associated with the ballad 'The Border Widow'.

Lament of the Border Widow

My love he built me a bonnie bower
And clad it all with lilie flower;
A brawer bower you ne'er did see
Than my true love he built for me.
There came a man by middle day,
He spied his sport and went away;
And brought the king that very night
Who brak my bower and slew my knight...
I took his body on my back
And whiles I gaed and whiles I sat;
I digged a grave and laid him in
And happed him with the sod sae green.
But think na ye my hert wis sair
When I laid the moul on his yellow hair?
O think na ye my hert wis wae
When I turned aboot awa to gae?
Nae living man I'll love again
Since that my lovely knight is slain;
With ae lock o his yellow hair
I'll chain my hert for evermair.

Andrew Lang describes this as the quintessential Yarrow ballad, 'fuller of pathos than all the countless pathetic ballads of Yarrow'. It is hard to know why so much sadness attaches to this beautiful valley, but comfort is at hand in the shape of Tibbie Shiel's Inn, a little further along the lochside.

Return to A708 and turn right (signed Moffat).

Tibbie Shiel's Inn sits on a narrow neck of land dividing St Mary's Loch from its mate the Loch of the Lowes. Here the formidable widow Tibbie accommodated and fed her six children and upwards of 30 overnighting travellers at a time in what was then a tiny cottage. This is a place to stop for a while to read the information boards in the inn car park and savour views that have changed little since Hogg's time, perhaps do 'The Ring of the Loch,' a family-friendly walking route, and then partake of Tibbie Shiel's hospitality. She, like Hogg, is at peaceful rest back in Ettrick kirkyard, after living to 96!

Alternatively, take a seat in the roadside cafe overlooking Tibbie Sheil's Inn and the lochs, in the company of a massive white statue of James Hogg who was a frequent visitor.

Leaving Tibbie Shiels, continue on A708 and proceed to the Grey Mare's Tail.

Continuing along the side of the Loch of the Lowes, and the winding roads beyond, yields spectacular mountain scenery rivalling the Scottish Highlands. This wild mountain country is steeped in Covenanter lore. Hogg set his novel of the Killing Times, *The Brownie of Bodsbeck*, at Chapelhope at the head of the loch. At Riskinhope nearby, James Renwick addressed his last conventicle before being apprehended and executed in Edinburgh's Grassmarket. And four Covenanters were summarily executed at Birkhill a few miles further on at the border of Dumfries and Galloway.

These were bloody times but beyond Birkhill is a spectacular waterfall, just visible from the road, which reminds us that nature carries on its work oblivious of human trials and triumphs. This is the Grey Mare's Tail which, along with the black tarn of Loch Skene in the hills above, can be accessed by foot from the National Trust car park at its foot. Also up there is a curious mound, long thought to be a giant's burial place. Archaeologists exposed this as a myth when they revealed that it had been an Iron Age enclosure. This is a place of interest to geologists, nature lovers, walkers, birdwatchers and an inspiration to artists and writers:

There eagles scream from isle to shore;
Down all the rocks the torrents roar;
O'er the black waves incessant driven,
Dark mists infect the summer heaven;
Through the rude barriers of the lake
Away its hurrying waters break,
Faster and whiter dash and curl,
Till down yon dark abyss they hurl.

So Walter Scott evokes the mood. Many scenes of his Covenanting novel *Old Mortality* are set in this wild landscape, a landscape through which he was guided on a mountain pony by James Hogg.

Turn around to return to Gordon Arms junction.

The route around the lochs and back to Yarrow Water allows fine views of St Mary's Loch and surrounding hills. Again, Scott captures the special something in landscape description within his narrative poem 'Marmion':

Abrupt and sheer, the mountains sink
At once upon the level brink;
And just a trace of silver sand
Marks where the water meets the land.
Far in the mirror, bright and blue,
Each hill's huge outline you may view.

Arriving back at the Gordon Arms, we return to a part of the valley that echoed with languages spoken by the Angles, the Celtic British tribes and others long forgotten. Archaeological finds in the area suggest higher levels of human activity before and after the Roman presence than elsewhere in the valley. Traces of cultivation terraces farmed by the British are still visible on hillsides around this meeting of roads and rivers and there is evidence of early Christian and older burials in the area.

There was some kind of violent confrontation here in the 6th century but who was fighting who and why is unclear. Was this a clash between warriors from Strathclyde in the west and the Selgovae who, after the Romans left, struggled to protect their lands from encroachment by other British tribes? Or was the conflict, as some believe, one of 12 fought by the legendary Arthur and his warriors to prevent Anglo Saxon invaders gaining control of the area, and then pushing north and west into the lands of the Picts and Scots?

At Gordon Arms junction continue on A708 (signed Selkirk).

Speculation also surrounds several standing stones lying at Annan Street between Yarrow Feus and Yarrow. Some are certainly more ancient than the events local lore attributes to them. The Yarrow Stone 50 metres or so up a path (signed Whitefield) marks the 6th century graves of two men. The inscription on the stone tells us they were Nudus and Dumnogenus, sons of Liberalis. Might they have fallen fighting alongside King Arthur or even have been related to him? Or are they, as has recently been suggested, Arthur himself and one of his warriors? Whoever they were, it is significant that these native British princes were given Christian burials and the site marked with an engraved stone.

The Glebe Stone a little further along the road, and the Warrior Stone in the garden of a cottage a little further again, make up the trio of larger stones. The former sits on the edge of moorland which was at one time peppered with mysterious cairns. The latter is close to a group of stone lined cists which were used for Christian burials following 'a scene of slaughter and sepulchre', but which also contained older artefacts.

This part of the valley's bloody reputation continued down the centuries. It was the scene of a bloody clash between feuding families, the bodies of the losers being thrown into 'dead man's lake'. And it may have been where, in 1616, Walter Scott of Tushielaw was waylaid and killed by members of Grizell Scott of Thirlestane's family for marrying without her father's consent. Once again, Walter's crime was not being of high enough status to be an acceptable suitor. Perhaps this was what cost the subject of the ballad 'Rare Willie' his life. First published in the mid-18th century it tells of a young woman's search for Willie who has gone missing,

> *Willie's rare, and Willie's fair,*
> *And Willies's wondrous bonny,*
> *And Willie vowed tae marry me,*
> *Gi'n e'er he married ony...*
> *O cam ye by the waterside?*
> *Pou'd ye the rose or lilye?*
> *Or cam ye by yon meadow green?*
> *Or saw ye my sweet Willie?*

Sadly, she finds him drowned in Yarrow. This ballad and another, the well-loved 'Dowie Dens of Yarrow', both exist in many versions and are perhaps themselves combinations of ballads.

The Dowie Dens of Yarrow

> *There was a lady frae the North*
> *She couldna find her marrow*
> *She was courted by nine gentlemen*
> *And a ploo boy lad frae Yarrow.*

The lowly suitor agrees to meet his more noble challengers to fight for his beloved's hand in marriage and, as was the protocol of the times, he opts to take on each of his opponents in one-to-one combat.

> *I'll no take a gun, a gun,*
> *I'll no take an arrow*
> *But I will tak a great broadsword*
> *To fight for you tomorrow.*

Faced with nine assailants, he kills five, wounds four but is fatally stabbed by his beloved's brother. The brother returns home to hear that his sister has had a premonition:

The lady said, 'dreamed yestreen —
I fear it bodes some sorrow —
That I was pu'in' the heather green
On the scroggy braes o' Yarrow.'
Her brother said, 'I'll read your dream.
But it should cause nae sorrow,
Ye may go seek your lover hame,
For he's sleepin' sound in Yarrow.'

Having gone to find her dead lover and brought him home, the grieving girl has a conversation with her less than sympathetic father:

'Go hold your tongue, ' her father said'
There's little cause for sorrow,
I'll wed ye on a better lad
Than ye hae lost in Yarrow.'
'Haud your ain tongue, my faither dear,
I' canna' help my sorrow;
A fairer flower ne'er sprang in May
Than I hae lost in Yarrow.'

John Veitch believed that the ballad records a young Mary the Flower of Yarrow's wish to marry a ploughboy not from Yarrow, but Gala. Walter Scott certainly believed it was about members of his family. Whether or not the ballad has its origins in a particular event matters little. The untimely loss of a young life is its tragedy.

That so many stories of this type have come down the ages in this area suggests love matches were rare. The message to young women was pretty clear – following your heart in defiance of parental plans for your future is likely to end in tears. And to young men aspiring to marry up the social ladder – if you value your life, watch your back!

Coming to Yarrow we pass Yarrow Kirk, built in 1640 after the Kirk of the Lowes at St Mary's Loch was destroyed by a fire started, it was alleged, by the Scotts to prevent their enemies, the Kerrs, seeking sanctuary there. Except for those few who lived at the top of the Yarrow, having a more accessible church must have been a relief – unless, of course, you were a Covenanter.

The Covenanters continued to trek up to St Mary's Loch or into the hills to worship at secret conventicles, especially after the restoration of the Stuart monarchy in 1660. From that date, Yarrow Kirk was staffed with ministers who ran services in the Episcopalian form imposed by Charles II rather than the Presbyterian way of the Covenanters. One minister of Yarrow Kirk, John Brenner, turned out to be a government informer whose reports led to raids on conventicles and several Covenanters being shot. In a retribution reminiscent of reiving times, he was himself shot.

Passing along the steep tree-lined left bank of the Yarrow, we pass Hangingshaw where the stronghold of the Murray family, the subjects of the Song of the Outlaw Murray, once stood. This ballad is unusual in that it is not about forbidden love, loss, revenge or heroic acts, but about the resolution of a dispute by reason and negotiation. It also throws light on why, in the medieval period, Borderers came to live their lives by their own code of law and honour rather than the king's.

The Ballad of Outlaw Murray

The Murray, with 500 men at his command, lived here comfortably in the 16th century. He was however declared an outlaw by James IV because he refused to acknowledge the king as his feudal superior. He claimed that he owned outright the lands his family had won back from English hands at some time in the past, presumably before the Normans arrived and introduced feudal forms of landholding, and was not obliged to acknowledge the king as his superior. The king, though, was determined to be acknowledged as overlord and so he sent an envoy to:

'Ask him of whom he holds his lands,
Or man, who his master may be
And desire him to come and be my man,
and hold of me yon forest free'

The envoy also carried a message that failure to comply would cost him his castle, his men – and his life. The envoy went back with the retort that:

'He says yon forest is his own
He wan it frae the Southronie (southerners)
Sae as he wan it, sae will he keep it,
Contrair all kings in Christentie'

The King then sent one of Murray's neighbours to summon him to a meeting:

'And gif he refuses to do that.
Bid him luke for nae gude o' me!
There sail nevir a Murray, after him
Have land in Ettricke Foreste frie.'

And still Murray refused. James IV insisted again but then decided a negotiated settlement was preferable to imposing his will by force. He therefore agreed to Murray's request that in exchange for acknowledging James as his feudal superior, the king should grant him the prestigious and hereditary title of Sheriff of Ettrick Forest. Well, that seemed a fair compromise to both and the deal was done. Murray, it appears, treated on an equal basis with the king and came out not only unscathed but handsomely rewarded.

Why was the king so magnanimous? Was it a PR stunt to get others claiming full ownership of land in the royal forest to acknowledge him as their feudal superior? Murray was not alone in asserting, in the absence of paperwork, that land in the royal forests was land they had won. By appointing Murray Sheriff of Ettrick Forest, the King was giving him more power but also the responsibility for ensuring his neighbours follow his example in acknowledging that the land they occupied was royal land held from the king their feudal superior. He was a smart man, James IV.

While James IV and Murray were engaged in reaching this mutually advantageous arrangement, tales of witches and strange happenings continued to circulate in this part of the Yarrow. Back up the valley on

Peatlaw, a local man was cutting peat one day when, overtaken by tiredness, he sat down to rest. Soon he was fast asleep and when he woke up in the same place many hours later he hurried home to tell them about a very vivid dream that involved flying. He must have had some explaining to do, because not only had he been gone all night but he had also come home without his jacket and cap. When he retraced his steps his jacket was on Peatlaw where he had lain down for a rest. His cap was nowhere to be found... until news arrived that it had been found hanging from the top of the church spire in the far distant town of Lanark! The fairies surely had taken him on an aerial trip!

And down in the Yarrow valley some nocturnal goings on came to light when the blacksmith's wife of Yarrowford was exposed as a witch.

The Blacksmith's wife of Yarrowford

The blacksmith of Yarrowford once took on two brothers as apprentices. They liked the work but as time went on the younger boy grew pale and thin and was more tired when he got up in the mornings than when he went to bed at night. Eventually, he told his big brother that every night he dreamed that the blacksmith's wife crept into their room and turned him into a horse by sliding a halter over his neck. Then she jumped on his back and rode him over the moors to a great hall where she tied him up and went into the hall to dance the night away. He awoke every morning, he told his brother, with sore legs and new bruises on his ribs.

The older boy was of course very concerned and suggested they swap beds. So the next night he got into his wee brother's bed and after a while, just as his brother said, in came the blacksmith's wife with a bridle, threw it over his head and, in an instant, he was a horse, saddled and ready to go.

On jumped the blacksmith's wife and off they went with her kicking his sides to make him go faster. When they got to a great hall, she louped off and tied him up to a hitching post. While she danced the night away, the horse used the time to rub his head on the wooden post until his bridle was so loose it fell off. Transformed into a human again, the lad grabbed the bridle and lay in wait.

When the blacksmith's wife eventually emerged from the hall the young man threw the bridle over her head and in an instant, she was a horse, he was on her back and they were homeward bound. This time however they stopped off at the forge long enough for the lad to put a new set of horseshoes on the horse.

That morning, there was no sign of the blacksmith's wife – and no breakfast. When the blacksmith went to find her there she was still in bed with the covers tucked under her chin. Thinking she must be ill he offered to bring the doctor. She however replied that there was no need for that and pushed back the covers to reveal horseshoes nailed to her hands and feet.

When the story had been told, the blacksmith took her off to Selkirk himself to hand her over to the authorities and be tried as a witch. And the wee apprentice? Well, he was nursed back to health by his big brother and the blacksmith who made sure he got the milk of cows put to graze in the churchyard – a familiar remedy for consumption.

As we near the junction of the Yarrow with the Ettrick, we pass Foulshiels and the shell of the cottage where Mungo Park the explorer was born. And just beyond, the top of 'a Ruin hoary' lours above the trees on the far side of the river. This is how Wordsworth described Newark Castle in 1814. Newark (New Work) Castle was built in the early 15th century to replace Auldwark, an older tower which was neither grand nor strong enough for the mighty Douglas family, since being granted extensive lands by Robert the Bruce in the early 14th century and the hereditary title of Keeper of the Forest. Sir Walter Scott chose Newark Castle as the setting for his epic poem 'The Lay of the Last Minstrel'.

At Bowhill Theatre / Ettrickbridge sign turn right, take right fork at first Y junction and right fork at second Y junction (signed Newark Castle).

Even cracked and roofless, Newark Castle still has the power to awe. With the steep river bank on one side and a three-metre-high wall, a barmkin, protecting the other three sides, it was considered invincible. In fact, it survived a siege and burning in the 1540s. When the Douglas family fell from royal favour in 1555 the castle was taken into royal hands and later granted to the Scotts of Buccleuch. They repaired but then abandoned Newark for the more comfortable predecessor of Bowhill House. It was, though, the scene of a bloodbath in 1645 after the Battle of Philiphaugh. The triumphant Covenanting forces brought their prisoners of war to Newark to await an escort to Edinburgh. But when the escort arrived there were no prisoners to escort. Their guards had given in to the urge to slaughter them as their royalist adversaries had done with Covenanters after previous battles. Those brave enough to venture up still hear ghostly cries on the anniversary of the battle.

Return to A708 and turn right (signed Selkirk) (Road beyond the castle not advised).

We join the road where the Yarrow is a smooth black surface one minute and a rush of sparkling white foam the next, tumbling through and over rocks as it goes to join the Ettrick at Carterhaugh. Leaving Yarrow, few would disagree with Wordsworth for whom the images of river, loch and valley lingered in the mind 'to heighten joy, and cheer my mind in sorrow'. He returned 18 years later to say goodbye to the gravely ill Walter Scott, and wrote:

Yarrow, through the woods,
And down the meadows ranging,
Did meet us with unaltered face,
Though we were changed and changing.

Ahead lies Philiphaugh, the low-lying area beside the Ettrick where the battle was fought. Montrose, the Royalist leader, and his troops chose Selkirk for an overnight stop on their way to Edinburgh. While he and his officers enjoyed the comforts of the town across the river, the infantry bedded down at Philiphaugh. News that they were there reached Leslie, the leader of a smaller army of Covenanters, who marched his men under cover of darkness to launch a surprise attack.

One local Royalist, Lord Traquair, was on his way to Selkirk with bags of coins to pay the royalist soldiers when he met them fleeing the battlefield pursued by the Covenanting army. Intent on saving his own skin, he persuaded a passing blacksmith to swap horses, and told him to hide the horse's saddle bags somewhere safe. The blacksmith reached home safely but without the bags. He had thrown them into a pond to lighten the horse's burden and make his own escape, he said. The fortune they contained has never been found.

At T junction turn right onto A707 (signed Selkirk) and follow signs for A7 Galashiels.

As we accompany the Ettrick on its journey to meet the Tweed, we give the last words on this journey to another Border poet, William Ogilvie.

Wild Ettrick, Wild Ettrick,
Your blue river gleams,
An azure cloak'd lover
That rides thro' my dreams,
The heath's at your stirrup,
The broom's at your knee,
You sing in your saddle
A love song to me.

Thro' green lands you led me
In lone ways apart
In long days you told me
Things dear to my heart,
In dream-time, in silence,
With haunting refrain
You murmur them over
And over again.

Wild Ettrick, Wild Ettrick
Love-raider in blue
Ah! Swing me to saddle

And take me with you
To glens of remembrance
And hills of desire,
The stars over Kirkhope
The Moon on the Swire.

Turn right onto B6360 (signed Abbotsford), and, reaching A6091 roundabout, follow signs to Tweedbank Station.

Journey 3
Tweeddale

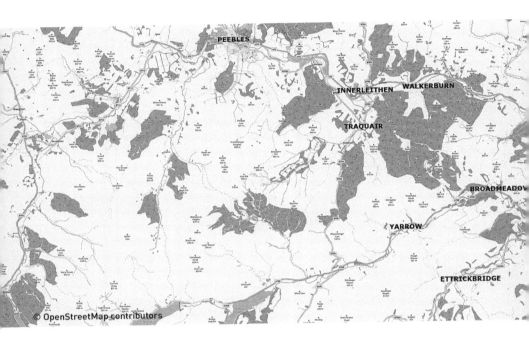

Journeying upriver we enter a rich history, some of which was written on the landscape by ancient peoples, some passed down in stories, and some in written records. The landscape changes as we move upriver westward to Drumelzier then southwest to reach the source of the Tweed, where, in Katrina Porteous' words, 'oozing from mud, glaur, rashes/Tweed begins to murmur never look back'.

The Tweeddale hills, now clad in grass and heather, were for many centuries green with trees. Peebles was the only town of any size, and, although Walkerburn and Innerleithen grew to be thriving mill towns in the 19th century, the area as a whole remained pastoral in character. Mediaeval Tweeddale was on the fringes of the cross-border tension and strife that plagued those who lived downstream. It had no abbeys and, after the Scottish Reformation outlawed Roman Catholicism, most of the churches simply carried on under new Protestant management.

In the Bronze and Iron Ages however Tweeddale was, by the standards of the time, a populous place and an important regional centre. Archaeological evidence tells of settlements dating as far back as 3,000 BCE and later of a strong Celtic presence. The Bronze Age peoples, the Celtic British tribes, the Romans and the Northumbrian Anglo-Saxons each in turn saw the importance of controlling this area. Why? Because the Biggar Gap on the north west edge of the Tweed valley led to the south west of Scotland, while the valleys of the Lyne and Meldon Waters linked it to the north. To control this area was to control the south of Scotland.

Besides its strategic importance, Tweeddale was also a cultural crossroads. Battles for minds and souls were played out here. Early Christianity came to the central and eastern Borders with evangelical monks like St Cuthbert who had links to Lindisfarne and were based in the first abbeys. The new faith came to Tweeddale from the west with peripatetic monks, notably, St Kentigern or Mungo. By the early mediaeval period the area was part of the diocese of Glasgow and reforming Scots-Normans were in charge. Their political and economic focus lay further east, which is perhaps why King David I built a castle but not an abbey at Peebles, and why the old ways and beliefs were so persistent. Despite Presbyterian efforts to eradicate these after the Reformation, and despite 17th century witch trials, burnings and drownings, the old beliefs lingered long in the minds and everyday lives of Tweeddale folk.

The ghosts, fairies, and wizards we meet in the myths and legends are echoes of both landscape and history. Over the centuries this heady combination inspired many to put pen to paper, some to mine the rich seams of stories running through the area, some to capture life as lived in their time and some to craft new stories. The area spawned literary giants and nurtured others who, although not born here, were drawn to and deeply affected by it.

As we travel up one side of the river and back down the other, we meet a playwriting monarch, Meg whose big mouth saved a life, a forgotten hero and Merlin Sylvestris, a wizard or druid and close associate of the legendary Arthur. And we hear how the Tweedie family got its name, why the ghost of a brokenhearted king haunts the hills, and why a set of gates are known as the 'steekit yetts'.

The Journey: 102–120 miles

From Tweedbank Station follow signs for A7 (signed Galashiels), cross the Tweed and take first exit at roundabout onto A7 south (signed Selkirk/Carlisle). At junction with B7060 turn right (signed Yair).

We leave the A7 where the Ettrick flows into the Tweed to follow in the tracks of the Celtic British as we round Rink Hill, so called for the Iron Age enclosure on the top. This enclosure, the largest north of the Cheviots, was positioned within sight of those on North Eildon and nearby Cauldshiels Hill across the Tweed. Each seems to have had a different function: North Eildon was designed for ceremonial and possibly political gatherings; Cauldshiels housed people, possibly fighting men; and the

Rink, judging by the enormous hauls of arrow heads and flint chippings retrieved here, specialised in making weaponry. Collectively, these hilltop centres might have been the Iron Age equivalent of a capital city.

Behind the Rink is the start of the enigmatic Catrail, a broken line of earthwork ditches and mounds running west then south across the hills towards the border with England. Its origins and purpose are as mysterious as Tim Douglas's lines suggest:

> *The earthwork is still in the top of the hill*
> *But what of the people who made it?*
> *The long-vanished race who once mastered the place*
> *Their unwritten history faded.*

More of the Catrail in other journeys, but for now enjoy the fine views up the Ettrick valley. This must surely have stopped many before us in their tracks.

At T junction at Yair Bridge turn right onto A707.

Still on the north side of the Tweed, we pass Fairnilee House close by the remains of Fairnilee Tower. This was the birthplace of Alison Rutherford, later Mrs Cockburn. She was the first of two 18th century Border women to write lyrics for an old tune, 'The Floo'ers o' the Forest', a lament for the Scottish men who died on the ill-fated Flodden Field in 1513. For this authoress however, her poignant words tell also perhaps of a private loss:

> *I've seen Tweed's silver streams,*
> *Glitt'ring in the sunny beams,*
> *Grow drumlie and dark,*
> *As they roll'd on their way;*
> *O fickle fortune!*
> *Why this cruel sportin?*
> *Oh! Why thus perplex*
> *Us poor sons of a day?*

Thy frown canna fear me,
Thy smile canno cheer me,
Since the flowers o' the forest
Are a' wede away.

Fairnilee also inspired Selkirk man Andrew Lang to weave strands of local legends, tales and history into his own tale, 'The Gold of Fairnilee' for his niece Jeanie in Australia: 'Your father and I have dug for treasure in the Camp of Rink, with our knives, when we were boys. We did not find it: the story will tell you why.' The tale features encounters with fairies and their magic, the ghostly figure of a man killed at Flodden seen riding past the family home before news of his death is delivered, and a baby accidentally scooped up with 'gear' captured in a cross-border raid who is raised with the reiver's other children – all things which are said to have happened at some time and place in Border history.

As we approach Caddonfoot, we could stop and put on walking boots to tramp over Meigle (or Margill) Hill as James Hogg, the Ettrick Shepherd did:

Lord Pringle sat on Margill brae,
Pondering on war and vengeance meet
The Caddon toiled in narrow way,
The Tweed rolled far beneath his feet.

Long before Hogg or Pringle tramped these hills, the Caddon valley twice played a part in Scotland's resolve to be an independent country. In 1018, Malcolm II, King of Scots, and Owain, King of Strathclyde, agreed to join forces to win back land north of the Cheviots occupied by the Northumbrians. Both summoned their men to Caddon Water and marched south to Carham and victory. In 1296, this was again a muster point for an army, this time with a plan to attack the English from the north while the French attacked from the south. On this occasion, the outcome was not favourable to Scotland – at the Battle of Dunbar, Edward I of England effectively, albeit temporarily, gained control of Scotland.

At Caddonfoot Bridge follow the road across the bridge to continue on A707. Cyclists may wish to leave the A707 a mile or so later to take the route along the south bank of the Tweed (signed Ashiesteil, Elibank, Traquair) and rejoin the route at Traquair House.

Ashiesteil House over on the south bank of the Tweed enjoys an intimate view of this secluded stretch of the valley. It so inspired Sir Walter Scott that, after he was appointed Sheriff of Selkirk, he rented the house from a cousin and then tried to buy it. We have his cousin's refusal to sell to thank for the existence of Abbotsford and Scott's later novels, since he mortgaged himself up to hilt to build it. Here at Ashiesteil however, he wrote his brilliant early works. Amongst these are the epic poems 'The Lay of the Last Minstrel', 'Marmion' and 'The Lady of the Lake'. Scott is said to have composed 'Marmion', his Romance of Flodden, in the woods. Every poem of the book begins with an evocation of the Tweedside seasons beginning with this wintry description of the Peel Burn ravine beside the house.

> November's sky is chill and drear,
> November's leaf is red and sere:
> Late, gazing down the steepy linn,
> That hems our little garden in,
> Low in its dark and narrow glen
> You scarce the rivulet might ken,
> So thick the tangled greenwood grew,
> So feeble trilled the streamlet through;
> Now, murmuring hoarse, and frequent seen
> Through bush and briar no longer green,
> An angry brook, it sweeps the glade,
> Brawls over rock and wild cascade,
> And foaming brown, with doubled speed,
> Hurries its waters to the Tweed.

Border lore has numerous stories of events foretold by those with prophetic gifts. Walter Scott himself had a premonition while he lived at

Ashiesteil. He was out riding with Mungo Park, then a doctor in Peebles, when the young man's horse stumbled. Mungo had just been telling Scott about his plan to return to Africa and continue the search for the source of the Niger. Interpreting the horse's stumble as a bad omen, Walter urged Mungo not to return to Africa. He shrugged off the advice saying 'Those as looks for freits, finds them'. Mungo left for Africa soon after – and did not return.

Travelling on, the picturesque ruin of Elibank Castle nestles at the edge of the Elibank and Traquair Forest over on the far bank.

Turn right at brown sign to visit Tweed Valley Forest Park Thornielee viewpoint.

In the early 17th century, Elibank was home to Gideon Murray, his wife and their three daughters. In an age when people were often identified by unusual physical characteristics, the oldest daughter was known locally as 'muckle-mou'ed Meg' on account of her larger than was fashionable mouth. A ballad tells the mostly true story in a not wholly accurate but entertaining way.

The Wife or the Wuddy

In the early 17th century, the legendary reiver Wat Scot of Harden and his family lived at Oakwood Tower across the hills in the Ettrick valley. His son, Will, was a handsome young man with a fine conceit of himself. He was keen to prove his reiving prowess to his father and so one moonlight night he set off over the hills with a band of men to steal cattle from the Murrays of Elibank, knowing them to be a family with which his folk had a long running feud.

Will and his men crept up to the castle, rounded up the cattle and set off over the hills with them. Disturbed cattle are noisy beasts, however, and Gideon Murray and his men were soon out of their beds and saddled up. They gave chase and caught up with the raiders, and as James Hogg recounts in 'The Fray of Elibank',

Soon weapons were clashing, and fire was flashing,
An' red ran the bluid down the Ashiestiel brae:
The parties were shouting, the kye they were routing,
An' rattling and galloping aff frae the fray.

Some died in the fracas but Will was taken captive and thrown into Elibank Castle's dungeon. Such was the enmity between the two families that Gideon fully intended to hang him in the morning rather than demand a ransom. However, when his wife Margaret heard who the captive was, the quick-witted woman reminded her husband that they had three unmarried daughters – and that the oldest was not particularly easy on the eye. As Hogg describes her,

Now Meg was but thin, an' her nose was lang,
An' her mou' it was muckle as ane could weel be;
An' her een they were gray, an' her colour was wan;
But her nature was generous, gentle and free.
Her shape it was slender, her manners refined,
Her shoulders were clad wi' her lang dusky hair,
An' three times mare beauties adorned her mind,
Than mony a ane's that was three times as fair.

And so Gideon offered Will Scott the choice of the gallows (the wuddy) or Meg's hand in marriage. Will Scott's initial reply was decidedly reluctant.

'Lead on to the gallows, then' Willie replied,
'I'm now in your power, an' ye carry it high;
Nae daughter o' yours shall ere lie by my side;
A Scott, ye maun mind, counts it naethin tae die.'

Will however asked for three days' grace to consider his options. Gideon Murray was of course happy to oblige. Whatever Will decided would be a winning outcome for the Murrays. By the end of those three days Will had decided that married life was preferable to no life and agreed to marry Meg.

In some versions of the story, it is Meg who buys Will time to reconsider. She pleads with her father to delay the execution and, when he grants her wish, she gets to work on a plan to change Will's mind. Posing as a servant girl she offers to take a message to his mother asking her to plead for his life. Meg delivers the message but no one comes to plead for Will's life, presumably because, besides leading his father's men to early deaths, he had been inept enough to get caught. However, as he is brought out of the dungeon to face his fate, Meg reveals that she is the kind servant girl and Will, touched by her kindness, or perhaps the prospect her dowry (the very cattle he came to steal), decides marriage might not be such a terrible fate.

> So Willie took Meg tae the forest sae fair,
> An' they lived a most happy an' social life;
> The langer he kend her, he lo'ed her the mair,
> For a prudent, a virtuous, and honourable wife.

Will Scott really did marry Meg, whose name was actually Agnes, but it seems he did so without any life-threatening inducements. That said, a second marriage contract had to be drawn up after the 20-week window for marrying after the first expired. Maybe some kind of persuasion *was* necessary. Whatever the reason, the couple lived a long and, by all accounts, happily married life, as the splendid wooden carving of a happy Meg and Will dancing at their wedding at this viewpoint suggests. They certainly produced many children.

Elibank was later associated with the Jacobite cause when, after the Jacobite defeat at Culloden in 1746, a Murray hatched a plot to kidnap the royal family in London and restore Bonnie Prince Charlie to the British throne. The 'Elibank' plot however came to nothing and Charles Edward Stuart died in disappointed exile.

It was the 5th Lord Elibank who responded to Dr Johnson's scathing comment that oats were food for horses in England and for men in Scotland, by saying 'Yes sir, and where will you find such men and such horses?' Quick thinking and an ability to speak one's mind was, it seems, an Elibank trait.

Return to A72, turn right (signed Peebles).

Travelling onward, we pass through Walkerburn and come to Innerleithen. We visit both on the return journey but head now to Traquair House, the oldest continuously inhabited tower house in Scotland.

Progress along Innerleithen High Street to junction with B709, turn left and follow signs to Traquair.

Traquair House, built on the site of a 12th century house, was once a royal hunting lodge. Still privately owned but open to the public, it has a romantic and unconventional history. After the Scottish Reformation, the family continued to espouse Roman Catholicism – a very risky thing to do. They had to worship in secret and, like Murray of Elibank, supported Bonnie Prince Charlie's bid to regain the British throne. In 1745, the Young Pretender stayed here on his way south with his Jacobite army and, as he left through the great gates, surmounted by sculpted bears, the Earl ordered the 'yetts to be steekit' (closed) until a Stuart monarch was again on the throne. To this day, the Bear Gates remain shut.

Charles' grandmother, Mary Queen of Scots, her husband Darnley and the baby who became James VI of Scotland and James I of England also stayed here. And it was to Traquair that the royalist Montrose came in 1645 seeking refuge after his army was routed by Covenanter forces at nearby Philiphaugh.

Traquair continues this tradition of offering a safe space with its annual 'Beyond Borders' festival. This event brings people together to share and exchange views and promote dialogue about situations of global conflict, inequality and injustice. In the past however, for reasons sadly familiar to those caught up in today's conflicts, people who should have been setting a good example took the law into their own hands. The first Earl of Traquair, aided and abetted by an outlaw, Christie's Will, did just that in the middle of the 17th century.

Bear Gates, Traquair

Christie's Will

The first Earl of Traquair was a Stuart who rose up through the social ranks in the reign of Charles I but ended his days as a beggar in Edinburgh after his king lost his crown and his head. In between, however, he was a powerful royal official and met one day with a reiving Armstrong – Christie's Will, as he was known, a descendant of the famous Johnnie Armstrong of Gilnockie. Only Will was locked up in Jedburgh's Jail. Asking why he was there, Traquair was told, 'for stealing twa halters'. This surprised the nobleman until Armstrong admitted that two fine horses had been attached to the halters. The amused Earl had Willie released.

Sometime later, Traquair became embroiled in a lawsuit about that endless Borders obsession – land. The case was to be heard before Lord Durie at the courts in Edinburgh, but the noble Earl got wind that Durie was likely to rule against him and decided to call in a classic Borders favour.

One morning Lord Durie was taking his regular early morning horseride along Leith Sands. He was hailed by another horseman who drew alongside and began to chat away affably but a few minutes later he was bundled off his horse, muffled in a cloak and carried off to be confined in a remote Borders dungeon.

A search commenced for the missing judge but without result. It was concluded that he had been washed out into the Firth of Forth leaving a riderless horse on the shore. Eventually, another judge was appointed who in due course heard the land dispute case, and ruled in Traquair's favour. Sometime later, a disorientated Lord Durie appeared at dawn on foot, at the very same spot from which he had vanished. Gradually his family and friends readjusted to his reappearance and he was reinstated to the bench. The land case was not however reopened.

Traquair later used Will Armstrong's services for demanding tasks such as bearing dangerous messages during the Civil Wars that followed. Armstrong continued his bold lawless ways but the Earl of Traquair paid for his loyalty to the Stuarts with personal ruin and the humiliation of life on the streets which, by all accounts, he endured with resilience and dignity.

Perhaps today's peaceful Traquair is better represented by a traditional love song 'The Bush Aboun Traquair'.

Will ye gang wi' me and fare
To the bush aboun Traquair?
Ower the high Minchmuir we'll up and awa,
This bonny summer noon,
While the sun shines fair aboun,
And the licht sklents gently doun on holm and ha.

Exiting Traquair, turn right onto B7062 (signed Peebles).

Passing the Bear Gates on the right, we carry on up the Tweed passing Cardrona, the site of yet another Roman camp and, on the hill above it, an Iron Age enclosure with the remains of a later tower house and Kailzie nearby. Reminders of Bronze Age settlements, Celtic enclosures,

Roman forts, fortlets and marching camps abound and the hillsides bear visible scars of ancient cultivation. We enter Peebles – to which we will return – to turn up the Manor Valley.

At the far end of Victoria Park turn sharp left (before the road forks at the bridge), turn right at sign for Cademuir/High School then left onto Bonnington Road (signed Cademuir). This road becomes single track with passing places.

Cademuir Hill had at one time three Iron Age hill enclosures. Later it became the muster point for soldiers drawn from the central Tweed and Yarrow valleys. Some historians believe the legendary Arthur and his warriors fought and won an important 6th century battle here. It was an important victory which thwarted Anglo Saxon ambitions to conquer Scotland. Although the area between the Cheviot Hills and the Firth of Forth did become part of the Kingdom of Northumbria for a time, Anglo Saxon ambitions to control the whole of Scotland were never realised.

Just after we cross a second cattle grid, the Manor Water trickles under the road, having journeyed from the top of Yarrow valley. Following it upstream by car, cycle or foot, takes us to remote places that draw travellers back again and again.

At T junction turn left and, at the top of the hill, left again (signed Manorhead) onto single-track road with passing places.

The Manor Valley is a world apart. Flanked by a mix of grass and scree-covered hills, scoured and scraped by the last Ice Age, the valley's bleak beauty rivals Ettrick and Yarrow. It too has a long history. A late 6th century stone memorial unearthed here commemorates Coninia, a woman of whom we know only her name, and that, according to the inscription, she was an early Christian martyr.

In Walter Scott's day, a man called David Ritchie lived a little way up the valley in what became known as the Black Dwarf's Cottage because David was the model for the main character in Scott's novel of that name. Born with exceptionally short legs, David's name lived on long after those who labelled him for his physical oddities and his eccentricities were forgotten. He was, though, the subject of gossip after his death. It was rumoured that after burial in Manor Kirk graveyard, his body had been disinterred by the 'resurrectionists' – grave robbers who, for a handsome fee, supplied bodies for the dissecting tables of Scotland's medical schools. The rumour was unfounded, but was sparked by signs of interference with the grave. David was in fact buried in two stages, his legs having been secretly taken to Glasgow for examination to discover why they were so short. The line between legitimate and criminal activity in pursuit of scientific knowledge and between fact and fiction was, in these days, a thin one.

Further up the valley a track on the right leads up a short distance to the site of Manor's original and very ancient kirk and to St Gordian's Cross, an early marker of Christianity: 'to the dead in Christ, who sleep in God's acre, St Gordian's Kirk, in peace'. Everything in the Manor is old and long-lasting, including the patterns of landholding that may go back to Celtic times.

Return to and continue past the Peebles via Cademuir junction and, after Manor Church, turn left at the cream cottage.

Passing between the stone gateposts to proceed up an unmade road to Barns Tower House, we enter the atmospheric setting that inspired John Buchan, novelist and later Governor-General of Canada, to write *John Burnet of Barns*, a historical novel which contains lyrical evocations of this landscape, based on Buchan's own memories:

> Often I would take my books and go into the heart of the hills for days and nights. It was glorious to kindle your fire in the neuk of a glen, broil your trout, and make your supper under the vault of a pure sky. Sweet, too, at noonday to lie beside the wellhead of some lonely burn, and think of many things that can never be set down and are scarce remembered.

John Buchan is a true poet of the remoter parts of Tweeddale, celebrating its moods, seasons and colours from 'delicate greenery' to brown torrent or white frozen blanket. As the hero John Burnet reflects, 'to my mind, there is a grace, a wild loveliness in Tweedside, like a flower garden on the edge of a moorland, which is wholly its own'. Buchan captures that elusive specialness – in Scots verse:

Yon are the hills that my hert kens weel,
Hame for the weary, rest for the auld,
Braid and high as the April sky,
Blue on the taps and green i' the fauld:
At ilka turn a bit wanderin' burn,
And a canty bigin' on ilka lea
There's nocht sae braw in the wide world' schaw
As the heughs and holms o' the South Countrie.

and in English lyric:

Down in the valley the sun is bright;
Hollows glow in the Autumn light;
But ever we dream of a brighter day
Over the hills and faraway.

One feels that the far travelled Buchan, politician and author, wanted most of all to be 'over the hills' in the faraway of Upper Tweeddale.

Returning to the road turn right and then left (signed Peebles via Cademuir) to return to Peebles.

As we journey back around Cademuir Hill, take a glance at Hallyards, the cream coloured house across the Manor Water. Adam Ferguson, historian, social and political philosopher, and father of sociology, lived here in his later years. He was a leading figure in the Scottish Enlightenment who formed a strong attachment to the Tweed valley. His ideas remain relevant. For example, he identified the origins of the 'corrosive forces of materialism' and the threat 'the bureaucratic machine' poses to democracy. He also emphasised the social value and importance of community. He would have been quite at home on a 21st century discussion panel. And without him, the Manor Valley would today be underwater. A plan to flood it for a reservoir to supply Edinburgh with piped water was rejected because of his opposition. The Talla and Meggat Water valleys were chosen instead.

Retrace your route to the junction with B7062 in Peebles, turn left and immediately right to cross Tweed, take second exit at the roundabout and park.

Peebles – meaning a place where tents are pitched – grew around the confluence of the Eddlestone Water and the Tweed. From humble beginnings, it expanded from the 11th century to become a Royal Burgh. Royalty and nobility with their retinues were frequent visitors to the town before 1603. The hunting was good and, like local folk from all walks of life, they were drawn to the town's annual fairs, especially the Beltane Fair in May. James I was a regular visitor and described the fair in 'Peblis to the Play', writing his poem in Tweedside Scots!

> At Beltane, when ilk body bounds
> To Peblis to the Play,
> To hear the singing and the sounds,
> Their solace sooth to say.

Later in the 15th century, the anonymous author of the 'Tale of the Three Priests of Peebles' has each priest tell a tale as they sit drinking wine around a roaring fire. The stories focus on the shortcomings of a weak king (possibly James III), the conduct of people in public positions and the sinful failings of Roman Catholic priests. The number three has significance in myth, legend and religion, and it seems in Peebles. Things came in threes in Peebles – three main streets, three churches, three gates into the town, three bridges and three 'e's in its name. A piece in Robert and William Chambers' weekly journal commented that the three salmon on the town's coat of arms had to be toasted with not one drink, but three. Consequently, 'as much superfluous liquor must have been shed in compliment to the three salmon as would keep the Tweed in flood for a week'. They would be bloggers now!

Robert Chambers was a geologist, historian and collector of Scottish tales and rhymes. He was also the anonymous author of a controversial 1844 book, *Vestiges of the Natural History of Creation*, which informed and preceded Darwin's *Origin of the Species*. He and his brother William had by this time established what became an internationally renowned publishing and printing business, devoted to educational works – notably, the multi-volume Chambers Encyclopaedia and Chambers Dictionaries. William's gift to Peebles of the Chambers Institute on the High Street is a statement of the value he put on making knowledge accessible. It now hosts an art gallery, a local history museum, and a museum devoted to John Buchan. Had the Brothers Chambers been born a couple of centuries earlier, they might have had an entirely different reputation: two bright questioning minds putting new-fangled ideas into folk's heads, both born with six fingers on each hand, would surely have been considered peddlers of the dark arts!

The town had its troubled times. It was attacked during the 14th century Wars of Independence and periodically after that, notably in 1549 during the nine-year war known as 'the rough wooing'. English troops burnt houses, farms and crops depriving people of food and incomes. Then there were repeated outbreaks of plague, and threats to economic stability and public order. By the early 17th century the Beltane horse races were banned because of 'quarrels, private grudges, and miscontentment between families'. And around this time the townspeople, as in other Border towns, found themselves battling in the courts, and sometimes more literally, to stop tenant farmers encroaching on the town's common grazing land – a battle they lost.

Times were particularly tough between the late 17th and early 19th centuries. Famines and changes in farming brought desperate people in from surrounding hills and further afield, seeking poor relief paid for by taxes on townspeople with money to spare. Happily, the town's fortunes revived with the coming of industry and the railways and, later, Peebles' reinvention as a fashionable spa town offering the health benefits of hydropathic treatments attracted visitors.

In the 20th century Peebles suffered in the two World Wars, confounding the perception that it is a douce place untouched by wider events. Eric Bogle, the Scots-Australian singer-songwriter born and raised in Peebles, summons up a more sombre mood in one of his most famous songs.

Did they beat the drum slowly?
Did they sound the fife lowly?
Did the rifles fire o'er you as they lowered you down?
Did the bugles sing 'The Last Post' in chorus?
Did the pipes play 'The Flowers o the Forest'?

Now, in the 21st century, it is a vibrant hub for creative arts and outdoor activities. Lord Cockburn's 19th century quip 'as quiet as the grave or as Peebles' certainly does not apply.

That Peebles reinvented itself more than once is down to those who kept the cauldron of Border history and stories simmering on the fire. Walter Scott, James Hogg, Robert Chambers, Andrew Lang, John Buchan and others supped from this pot and added to it. However, another of Peebles' sons, John Veitch, was the first to blend all of these ingredients. A writer and avid collector of poetry, he climbed the academic ladder to hold chairs in logic, metaphysics and rhetoric at St Andrews and Glasgow Universities. His fascination with the influence of landscape on poetry led him to write his two-volume *History and Poetry of the Scottish Border*. It was a labour of love which proved his most lasting legacy – which might have surprised and pleased him!

Return to the roundabout at Tweed bridge, take second exit onto A72 (signed Glasgow) then, at the brown sign for Cross Kirk, turn right onto Young Street and follow signs to Cross Kirk.

In the 13th century, King Alexander III was visiting when the bones of St Nicholas and an ancient cross were found nearby. Hearing of the miracles ascribed to these bones, he founded Holy Rood or Cross Kirk to house them. Although surrounded now by houses, this atmospheric ruin remains a place of tranquillity.

Return to A72, turn right and exit Peebles.

The road out of town passes the reconstructed 12th century St Andrews Tower then climbs to Neidpath Castle, perched on a crag overlooking the Tweed. It dates from the 15th century but the original was built by Gilbert Fraser who also had strongholds upriver at Oliver and Fruid. This Norman lord was enticed north by David I with promises of land in the late 11th century. One of his descendants played a significant but largely forgotten part in Scotland's story.

A Forgotten Hero

The names of William Wallace and Robert the Bruce are remembered as the 'Braveheart' defenders of Scotland's independence. John the Graham, the Good Sir James Douglas and Thomas Randolph often rate a mention, but few except true Borderers remember Symon Fraser of Neidpath and Oliver. Yet the Frasers, or Frisels, were the greatest Barons of Tweeddale and key supporters of royal government. The father of our Symon was Sherriff of Peeblesshire and Keeper of the Forests of Selkirk and Traquair, and a notable patron of Melrose Abbey. Like many in the upper ranks of Scotland's nobility, the Frasers trod cautiously during the succession crisis at the end of the 13th Century, and Symon's father did homage to Edward I of England.

However, when Edward's intention to subordinate Scotland became clear, the young Symon took up the national cause. Captured at the siege of Dunbar Castle, he escaped and got his lands back by doing military service for Edward in Flanders. However, on his return to Scotland, Fraser switched sides. The young Borderer just could not stand on the side lines, having watched the archers of Selkirk Forest fight heroically in William Wallace's schiltrons only to be cut down by superior armour and numbers at Falkirk.

Fraser, now himself Keeper of the Forest of Selkirk, had everything to lose by joining the patriotic resistance. However, as a faithful son of the Church, he may have been swayed by the Pope's ruling in favour of Scotland's claim to national status against Edward's assertion of England's superiority. Whatever the reason, Fraser with his knowledge of the lie of the land and how to disappear into remote glens, aided William Wallace in his guerrilla resistance.

In 1305, with Scottish strength waning, William Wallace was betrayed and cruelly executed in London. But Robert the Bruce took up the national cause and he too had the support of Symon Fraser. Indeed, Symon saved Bruce's life when they were ambushed at Methven in Perthshire by getting him back on his horse three times and away. He himself however was captured shortly after the Methven debacle, taken to London and hung, drawn and quartered as if a traitor. His severed head joined Wallace's on display at London Bridge.

In the damning words of the gentle scholar John Veitch, Edward's true character 'was shown in the cruel execution of Symon Fraser, when no purpose was to be served except the gratification of limitless revenge'. Edward's dying instruction that his skeleton should be borne before an invading army until Scotland was finally conquered remained unfulfilled thanks to heroes such as Symon Fraser of Neidpath.

The male Fraser line expired with Symon and the properties and land passed to his daughter. Neidpath Castle remained invincible until the mid-17th century when Cromwell's' troops occupied Peebles and captured it. Sadly, the Neidpath woods were more vulnerable, being savagely culled in 1795 by the decadent fourth Douglas Duke of Queensberry, leaving the old Tower, in Wordsworth's furious denunciation 'beggared and outraged!' Fortunately, these lovely banks are again tree clad. Many historical events and legends are associated with the castle and its many owners. The saddest is the tragic tale of the 'Maid of Neidpath'.

The Maid of Neidpath

Lady Jean Douglas of Neidpath and Walter Scott, the young laird of Tushielaw in the Ettrick valley, met and fell madly but inconveniently in love. He was well below her in social status and so they had to meet in secret. Jean's father read the signs and, catching them together one day, had young Walter run out of the area. Walter signed up as a soldier and went off to fight but Jean, left alone, pined for him. Indeed, she was wasting away before her father's very eyes. Such was his concern for her life that when he heard that young Walter had returned from war safely, he invited him to call at Neidpath on a particular day.

Jean was ecstatic and, on the appointed day, dressed in her best clothes and insisted on going to Peebles to wait on the balcony of her father's town house on the High Street for her beloved to ride into town, spot her and come to claim her. Tragically, in his haste to reach Neidpath, Walter did not see the pale bone-thin woman waving from her balcony as he galloped his horse along the High Street. Or perhaps he did see her but, now a shadow of her former lovely self, he did not recognise her.

The shock was too great for poor Jean. She collapsed and died of a broken heart. To this day, she haunts Neidpath Castle, banging doors in displeasure when she hears sounds of merriment.

Neidpath's stories resonate long after we leave, a feeling captured by Mhairi Owens in her poem, 'Keep', the original whole of which is laid out in the shape of Neidpath Castle itself. She describes it as:

Rising still from the rock cliff
a tower over this gully of the black dwarf and fairy rings...
There is compulsion some unreadable countenance in that
    expressionless facade
Maybe there is left magic to be had behind those slit eyes.

Beyond Neidpath the road wriggles along to reach the junction with the Lyne Water which picks up the Meldon burn flowing from the north shortly before it reaches the Tweed. And in the cleft of the rivers is Sheriff Muir, a muster point for the Peebles militia into the 18th century.

Archaeology shows that this river junction, accessible from every direction, was for several millennia a populous place. There were standing stones, a communal burial site dating back to 4,000 BCE, and a large cluster of buildings known to archaeologists as the Lyne Ceremonial Complex. Amongst the structures is an enormous Iron Age enclosure which, like the one on Eildon Hill North, had ceremonial as well as military, political and economic functions. Groups of the Celtic Selgovae may have converged here to pay homage to chiefs and tribute in the form of cattle. And, as downriver, the Romans established camps and fortlets close by. These housed upwards of 1,000 men, their horses, and enough people to keep them all fed, watered and entertained.

Beyond the junction with the B712 is Lyne Kirk and, nearby, the outline of a Roman fort overlooks the confluence of the Lyne with the Tweed. There has been a church on this site since the 12th century. There may have been an even earlier church behind it on Abbey Knowe, where some very early Christian graves have been found. It is an evocative place to stand and think of those who also passed this way and the beliefs that shaped them.

Return to A72 /B712 junction and turn right (signed Drumelzier/Broughton).

Travelling upstream we come to Stobo, and another ancient kirk, this one reputedly founded in the 6th century by St Kentigern alias St Mungo. The medieval ties with Glasgow Cathedral were so strong that people said that Stobo belonged 'to God, St Mungo, and the Bishop of Glasgow'. A stained-glass window here depicts St Kentigern converting Merlin Sylvestris, of whom we hear more shortly, to Christianity. The window is a reminder that while the Celtic British chiefdoms, and later the Angles of Northumberland, battled for control of the area, another fight was taking place for souls torn between the old beliefs and Christianity. Support for Christianity waxed and waned for the best part of a millennium until, by the 12th century, Christianity emerged as the dominant belief system, publicly at least.

Coming to Dawyck, now in the care of the Royal Botanic Gardens, we pass through land owned between the 12th and 17th centuries by the Veitch family. The Veitches, and their neighbours the Tweedies, lived for generations in a state of almost permanent feud with each other. Like many other families of the time, they lived by an honour code that required that slights be answered directly and death summarily avenged. James VI and I stepped in to halt an escalation of the violence between these two families after the Veitches killed John Tweedie to avenge the ambush and murder four days previously of Patrick Veitch whose father had refused to pay the tolls the Tweedies levied for crossing their lands.

The presumption on the part of the Tweedies that they could settle things without recourse to the courts, arose because, for a century, they had literally got away with murder. In a feud with the Flemings in the early 16th century over whose son should marry Catherine Fraser, the heiress of nearby Fruid, James Tweedie killed John Fleming. Despite the gravity of the crime, the court banished him for three years and ordered his father to build a church at Biggar and fund prayers for the soul of the murdered man. John though returned to Scotland before the three years were up, and got the girl and her estate. Rough justice for the Flemings! But John Fleming's son had his revenge for his father's murder – he blew up Tinnis Castle, the main Tweedie family stronghold upriver above Drumelzier.

A local legend, retailed by Walter Scott, tells how the Tweedies got their name. Sometime in the early middle ages, an elderly Tweeddale baron went off to the Crusades leaving behind his beautiful young bride. When he returned, he was greeted by a child who, to his surprise, called his wife 'mother'. By way of explanation, she told him that she had been walking by the river when a man emerged from a deep pool (now the Devil's pool), saying he was the guardian of the river. He had, she said, seduced her and nine months later she gave birth to this beautiful, apparently human, little boy. The elderly Baron accepted this explanation and raised the child, who was already known locally as Tweedie, as his own. The more prosaic truth is that King Alexander III granted land on the Tweed to a man who signed as Johannes de Tueda at a time when men often took their name from the place they lived.

And so to Drumelzier. Here the Biggar water joins the Tweed from the north and the Drumelzier alias Powsail Burn from the south. This, like other river junctions, was a busy place in times gone by. Beside Dreva Crag, one of several Celtic enclosures and settlements, there is clear evidence of a field system which was very advanced for its time. This was no backwater! Tradition however remembers this riverside location because of its most famous visitor.

The Wild Man

Merlin, also known as Merlin Sylvestris (of the woods), or in Christian sources Myrdin Wyllt, meaning Wildman, is buried here. Although Merlin and his association with Arthur and the Round Table is well known, the historical facts are distinctly hazy. Debate continues about where Arthur's 12 battles against Anglo Saxons attempting to take over Celtic British territory were fought.

Merlin however is widely attested in Celtic and medieval lore as a wizard, a bard and a seer, and, as such, an important adviser to Arthur during military campaigns. It is also known that at one time he roamed the forests of upper Tweeddale half crazed, after the British army he was accompanying, or perhaps leading, was heavily defeated on Liddel Water.

Towards the end of his life Merlin met St Kentigern who, as the stained-glass window in Stobo Kirk depicts, persuaded him to become a Christian. He was buried close to where the Powsail joins the Tweed after he died. He foretold his own threefold death – by beating, drowning and stabbing – a prophecy which proved to be uncannily accurate. He was set upon and stoned by local shepherds, possibly because he was behaving strangely or maybe because word had got around that he had rejected their beliefs in favour of Christianity. Then he was pushed into the Tweed, where he fell on stakes the fishermen had placed to catch salmon, and then he drowned.

Much later, Thomas the Rhymer, also a seer, foretold that 'When Tweed and Powsail meet at Merlin's grave, Scotland and England one monarch shall have'. And so it was that on the very day when James VI of Scotland was crowned James I of England in 1603, the Tweed flooded and met the Powsail Burn. What were the odds of that?

Today, Drumelzier Church still sits on an ancient Christian site, and starting from the path on the right hand side of the kirkyard gate, visitors or pilgrims can follow the short path down to the thorn tree enclosure that marks Merlin's grave.

The confluence of the Powsail or Drumelzier Burn with the Tweed has almost certainly moved since Merlin's time. Old beliefs, however, were deeply embedded, even after Calvinism had outlawed both pre-Christian and Roman Catholic practices. These had co-existed relatively happily in the minds of many people up till then. Indeed, as a local tale of an encounter with fairies suggests, belief in the supernatural world of fairies continued after the Reformation as it did elsewhere in the Borders.

The Fairies of Merlin's Crag

One day a local man was sent to dig peats for his master's fire. Off he went to a rocky outcrop called Merlin's Crag which was close to a good bed of peat. He was digging away and thinking he might take a few extra peats for his own family when a wee woman appeared from nowhere and started yelling at him.

'What do you think you are doing?' she shouted and went on 'How would *you* like it if I ripped the roof off your cottage? Put that back right now... or else...'

Or else what? Who is this wee woman? And then it dawned on him. She must be one of the fairy folk and if there was one thing he was sure of, no good could come of upsetting her. So he put the turf back and patted it down with his spade. When he looked round the wee woman had gone.

Back he went to the farm empty-handed and, of course, when he told the farmer what had happened, he didn't believe him. He thought he was shirking or, worse, that he'd got his hands on strong drink. 'Fairies my foot! Get back up that hill tomorrow and bring back peats if you want to keep our job,' he said. Well, the man had a young family to support so the next day he went back and started digging. This time he got the job done with no interruptions.

A year or so later, the man was passing Merlin's Crag on his way home at dusk with some milk the farmer had given him for his family. Overtaken by a wave of tiredness, he lay down beside a wee hillock of grass and shut his eyes. After a while he heard music and opened his eyes to see that he was surrounded by fairies. They were dancing round him and beckoning him to join in. 'Why not!' he thought and joined in. He wasn't a great dancer but they seemed happy to dance with him. On and on they danced and before he knew it they had danced the night away and it was nearly dawn.

As the first cock crowed the fairies stopped dancing, grabbed him by his hands and ran off towards Merlin's Crag. There, to his amazement, a door opened in the hillside. In they went and at the end of a passage out they came into a big hall. And waiting for them there was the wee woman who had given him such a row for taking the roof of her house. Now he was worried! What was she going to do? He *had* taken peats from the hill despite her warning. But all she did was smile and say that he could go home on condition that he told no one what he had seen in the fairies' subterranean home. He breathed a sigh of relief and off he went. As he passed the grassy hillock he spotted the milk he had been taking home. He sniffed it – yes, it was still fresh – and headed for home. What a tale he had to tell them!

When he opened the door of his cottage he couldn't believe his eyes. There was his wife, but she had aged, and was surrounded by a bunch of teenagers! And they were all staring at him. Eventually his wife said 'Where have you *been* these seven years?' Not surprisingly, she didn't believe his explanation. After all, no jug of milk could stay fresh for seven years. The fairies had their revenge for the damage he did to their roof after all.

Continue on B712 to junction with A701, turn right (signed Broughton/Edinburgh) and proceed to Broughton.

A short detour north takes us to Broughton, below the Dreva hillfort. The village boasts an ancient church of St Llolan – a ruin above the north end – and in its centre the Broughton real ale Brewery. Also at the north end is Broughton House which was the home of a leading Jacobite, John Murray, who became Bonnie Prince Charlie's Private Secretary. Unfortunately, 'Secretary' Murray later became notorious as 'Evidence' Murray when, after the 1745 Jacobite Rising, he turned King's Evidence, so betraying many of his former comrades. This happened when Murray, who had lived rough in the Highlands like his Prince, was hunted down here in his home country. He took refuge at nearby Kilbucho House, and then finally lay low at Polmood up the Tweed where he was captured. Walter Scott recounts how his very un-Jacobite lawyer father, who had Murray as a client, would throw the teacup used by the turncoat out of the window when he had left, declaring 'Neither lip of me or of mine comes after Mr Murray of Broughton's!'

Returning to junction with B712 continue upriver on A701 south (signed Moffat).

This landscape was once swathed in the trees of the Royal Forest of Tweedsmuir, a favoured royal hunting haunt. On the left is Stanhope and then Polmood, once a royal hunting lodge granted to Norman the Hunter in a charter with the following wonderful wording:

> I, Malcolm Kenmure King, the first of my reign, gives to the Normand Hunter of Powmood, the Hope, up and down, above the earth to Hell as free to thee and thine as ever God gave it to me and mine, and that a bow and broad arrow when I come to hunt in Yarrow, and for the mair suith I bite the white wax with my tooth, before thir witnesses three, May, Mauld and Marjorie.

Perhaps in something of the same spirit, James Hogg sets an uproarious farce here in the time of James IV, entitled 'The Bridal of Polmood', in which everyone including the King and nobles are ridiculed. Suspicion lingers that this is Hogg's bawdy, insubordinate riposte to the stylized, up-market Romanticism of Walter Scott's 'Marmion' set in the same period.

A little beyond Polmood the meagre remains of Symon Fraser's Oliver Castle can be traced on the right, and directly opposite on the left, Tweedsmuir village and church. John Buchan was so influenced by time spent with his grandparents here that he took the name Lord Tweedsmuir when he was made a peer. The main attraction of Tweedsmuir today is as the starting point for heading on foot into the higher Borders hills above Talla and Fruid reservoirs.

The wilds of Upper Tweeddale and the Yarrow valley again became royal hunting grounds in the 1680s but this time Covenanters were the prey. They were so called because they signed a 1638 Covenant setting out their reasons for refusing to accept royal interference in how Scottish Presbyterians worshipped and organised. In the 1680s, the Stuart kings Charles II and James VII of Scotland and II of England sent troops to hunt Covenanters. In the churchyard at Tweedsmuir a gravestone erected many years after the death in 1685 of a local Covenanter is witness to this shameful religious intolerance. It reads: 'Here lies the body of John Hunter martyr who was cruelly murdered... for his adherence to the word of God and Scotland's covenanted work of the Reformation'. Another stone in the Tweedsmuir Kirk graveyard is a poignant reminder of the human cost of Edinburgh's plentiful supply of clean water. It commemorates the lives of over 30 men who died, and were buried here, during the building of the Talla Reservoir between 1895 and 1905.

Continuing upriver we come to where a royal love story ended in tragedy. It concerns Kenneth the Grim, who was supplanted as king of Scots by Malcolm Kenmure, the same Canmore mentioned in the Polmood Charter.

Bertha of Badlieu

Once when staying at Polmood, Kenneth followed the chase upriver into the high fells. There a great mist rolled down, blanketing the land, and Kenneth lost his way back into the valley. He was relieved to see lights in a rude cottage and went to seek shelter. When the door was opened to the bedraggled king he was astonished to be greeted by the most beautiful young woman on whom he had ever set eyes.

This was Bertha of Badlieu, daughter of a poor herdsman, whose wife had died in childbirth leaving this one girl. The ageing king fell immediately and deeply in love. He came often to the remote hut. After a while the herdsman agreed to let his daughter live at Polmood as the king's mistress. There she gave birth to at least two children, providing happiness and warmth to the life of a king beset with many troubles.

Not least of these was Kenneth's haughty Queen. When she heard of the lovely young peasant woman residing in her husband's oft visited hunting lodge, she feared that she and her son might be displaced from the royal succession. And she nursed her resentment till it cankered.

Meanwhile Kenneth had to go north to resume hostilities with the Norse raiders who were assailing Scotland at this time, hungry for plunder, trade and land to settle. After one such campaign, Kenneth returned eagerly to Polmood, only to find the place devastated, its occupants butchered.

'What happened?' groaned Kenneth in his anguish, and the reply, in storyteller Jean Lang's version, comes from an old servant who had survived the massacre:

> 'I thocht ye wad ken. Your Queen sent murderers wha slew them aa
> – the auld man, the bit bairns, and Bonnie Bertha o' Badlieu. They
> howkit a grave for them here on the hillside, and here they lie.'

Kenneth was a broken man and lost all interest in ruling Scotland. A weak king is as bad as no king and eventually he was killed by his ambitious cousin

Malcolm who also killed Kenneth's remaining sons and took the throne for himself.

This story however has an ironic twist. Kenneth's granddaughter Gruach married MacBeth. As Lady MacBeth, she goaded her husband to murder Duncan, grandson of the ambitious Malcolm, so regaining the throne for Kenneth's line – and giving Shakespeare his play. Meanwhile, the ghosts of Kenneth and Bertha wander the hills at the source of the Tweed, tragically unable to see each other and reunite.

The road continues past Badlieu towards 'Wells o' Tweed', where in the words of poet Tim Douglas, lies 'a moorland well, half-hid by rushes green, fringed with forget-me-not and meadow-bloom', yet 'a thing of power, its gathering waters loom'.

Turn around and return to Tweedsmuir.

There is a choice of routes to Innerleithen, our next stop. Both offer grand views of a landscape that John Veitch described as 'a sea of hills whose tops move and yet do not move for they carry our vision along in an undulating flow'.

EITHER follow A72 back to Innerleithen OR turn right at the sign for Talla and Fruid to return on single track road with passing places and some steep ascents to join A708 at St Mary's Loch. Turn left at the Gordon Arms Hotel onto B709 (signed Innerleithen). From Innerleithen High Street follow brown signs to St Ronan's Wells.

Innerleithen owes its existence and fortunes almost entirely to water. The mineral rich spring water feeding the Doo Well has quenched many a thirst. Indeed, it became a holy well and was later renamed St Ronan's Well in honour of the 8th century monk who caught the Devil with the crook of his staff. Not only did he 'cleik' the Devil but St Ronan gave him such a drubbing with the staff that he ran off and kept going until he was well out of the area. This scene is re-enacted every July at the Cleikum Ceremonies during St Ronan's Games, a ten-day festival of sport which culminates in 'Burnin the Deil', a fireworks display set off from nearby Caerlee Hill. There two millennia ago, the Celtic British would have lit their ritual fires in the Iron Age enclosure.

From the late 18th century, people flocked to St Ronans to 'take the waters' and bathe in the health-restoring waters, among them local celebrities James Hogg and Walter Scott. This popular spa town became even more fashionable after Scott wrote *St Ronan's Well*, the only one of Scott's novels set in his own time. The enterprising owner of Traquair House then extended facilities around the spring.

At the height of the spa's popularity, Alexander Brodie, a humble blacksmith from Traquair who made a fortune in London, spent a whopping £3,000 on building and equipping the first textile mill in Innerleithen. Touchingly, his venture was motivated not by a desire to make money but a wish to help those no longer able to find agricultural work. Brodie's Mill did give work to many who would otherwise have had to leave the area but it was not a commercial success. Nonetheless, harnessing the Leithen Water's power caught on and Innerleithen became a major producer of woollen textiles.

Return to A72, turn left and, at the other end of the High Street, left onto Leithen Road (signed golf course) to park near brown sign for The Pirn for optional walk.

The Pirn, where seven Iron Age huts once stood, hosts Mary Kenny's sculpted sandstone panels. These offer a glimpse into the life and minds of those who lived within this protected enclosure – a fitting place from which to view the dramatic sweep of our Tweeddale Journey.

Return to A72 and turn left.

Back on the A72, we pass through Walkerburn, a mill town named for the rushing stream to which it owes its existence and follow signs for Galashiels. The A72 leaves the Tweed at a roundabout just beyond Ashiesteil at the spot which inspired Andrew Lang to write the 'Ballade of the Tweed', which tells us why this stretch of water is special to him:

There's mony a water, great or sma',
Gaes singing in his siller tune,
Through glen and heuch, and hope and shaw,
Beneath the sunlicht or the moon:
But set us in our fishing shoon
Between the Caddon burn and Peel,
And syne we'll cross the heather broun
By fair Tweedside, at Ashestiel!

As an enthusiastic fisherman, he also denounces those responsible for polluting the river:

Deil tak the dirty trading loon
Wad gar the water ca' his wheel,
And drift his dyes and poisons doun
By fair Tweedside, at Ashestiel!

The final leg of our journey takes us by Clovenfords and Galashiels into the commercial and industrial world that so upset Lang and others who saw, from a privileged perspective, how costly to the environment these new technologies were. Clovenfords, so called because it leads to two ancient fords across the Tweed, was until the 20th century, on the main route from Edinburgh to Carlisle. The inn, a stopping off place for travellers, did a steady trade especially when Walter Scott lived at Ashiesteil.

Leaving Clovenfords, the road curves around Meigle Hill. The Meigle Pots, mysterious indentations left in the landscape by retreating glaciers at the end of the last ice age, were a favoured place for Covenanters in the middle decades of the 17th century until, that is, the greatly feared John Graham of Claverhouse, or 'Bluidy Clavers' as he was known, surprised a conventicle here in 1679. The minister was imprisoned but, unlike the Covenanters commemorated in the churchyard at Tweedsmuir, those captured here got off with fines, perhaps because they were mainly women and of middling social rank.

Now, the road drops down into the valley of Gala Water, to Galashiels, and the start of another journey.

Proceed through Galashiels following signs for A7 (signed variously Melrose, Selkirk, Langlee), then at roundabout on edge of town A68/A6091 (Jedburgh) return to Tweedbank Station.

Journey 4
Galawater, Wedale and Lauderdale

Leaderfoot Viaduct
Shutterstock

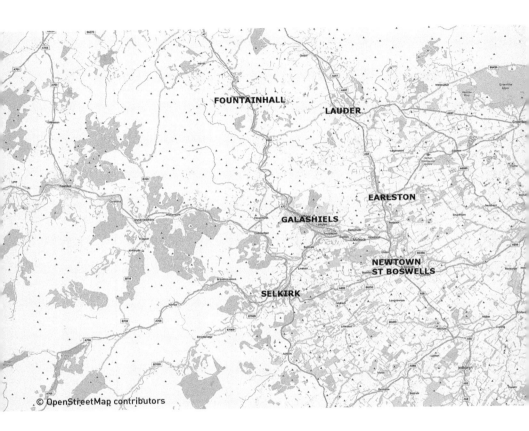

© OpenStreetMap contributors

North of the Tweed we travel up the Gala Water and down the Leader Water. The two rivers are hemmed in by hills to the west and east and so most travellers used, as now, these river valleys and the hills between them. Routes ran close to and beneath today's roads or walking paths. The drove roads for cattle and the Herring Road from the coast, criss-crossed the hills to connect with them.

The numerous Celtic British hill enclosures, Roman fortlets and camps, and the tower houses that later lined these routes indicate that defence of this narrow corridor mattered greatly to whichever overlord had control. The need for military defence waned after the Union of the Crowns in 1603, disappearing with the Union of the Parliaments in 1707, but even before then life on this side of the Tweed was generally more peaceable than to the south – not least in the centuries after David, Earl of Northumbria, was crowned David I of Scotland in 1124.

For most of this time Wedale and Lauderdale folk shared the hills with thousands of sheep belonging to one or other of the Border Abbeys. Until the abbey lands passed into private hands after the Reformation, relatively little land was held by non-monastic tenants. At some distance from the border with England there was also less threat from marauding armies. While the reiving dynasties south of the Tweed were stealing cattle from one another and carrying out cross border raids, the people of Lauderdale gained an early reputation for settling disputes through the courts. That is not to say that life in Wedale and Lauderdale was uneventful or that all conflicts were resolved bloodlessly. There were battles and family feuds, but these were usually sparked by political events and religious differences.

Things were less peaceful before the arrival of monastic flocks. In the 7th century, the Anglo-Saxon Northumbrians wrested control of the lands between the Tweed and the Firth of Forth from the Celtic British. Physical and diplomatic tussles for control continued until a mid-10th century deal was struck. This merged several kingdoms to create England, relinquished the lands north of the Tweed to the Scots, and reduced the Kingdom of Northumbria to an earldom. By the time David was crowned King of Scotland, the border had settled along the Cheviots and the eastern end of the Tweed.

So, for nearly five centuries, the people who lived in Wedale and Lauderdale were either on the edge of the Kingdom of Northumbria or outside it. This may explain why Anglo Saxon influence on place names and settlement patterns here is minimal and why English replaced Cymric, the language of the Celtic British, more slowly than south of the Tweed. The area was also until the 19th century more sparsely populated than lands to the south. These continuities may explain why a Galashiels accent is still distinguishable from accents heard in nearby Selkirk, Melrose and Peebles.

Travel in and out of these parts was not undertaken lightly before toll-funded turnpike roads and bridges connected Edinburgh with Carlisle and Jedburgh in the late 18th century. Roman Dere Street was repaired periodically to serve as a military route, but generally roads were rough tracks and frequently impassable. And there was the added challenge of getting across the Tweed. There were few bridges and in fact, for a long time, none between Peebles and Kelso.

And so, for millennia, these dales grew men for fighting, cattle and, latterly, sheep. Although the abbeys sowed the seeds of the textile industry that transformed the central Borders in the 19th century, government policies to reduce reliance on imported goods and maximise exports created the conditions for growth. Skilled textile workers were enticed from abroad with promises of tax breaks and special privileges, and steps were taken to stimulate and protect domestic production (for example by insisting Scots had by law to be buried in a shroud of Scottish linen). By the 1770s, the country had a sizeable textile industry. The mechanisation of spinning and weaving processes over the next 50 years revolutionised production and transformed the small, unremarkable burgh of Galashiels into a dynamic industrial town exporting high quality cloth across the globe.

This meteoric rise was lent some serendipitous aid by literary neighbours, Sir Walter Scott and James Hogg. They popularised the distinctive shepherd's check pattern and later tartan. The association of woven woollen cloth with the area was further strengthened through the misreading by a clerk of 'tweel' (an alternative term for twill) as 'tweed'. Whether this came about as a consequence of bad handwriting or poor eyesight is unknown but the name stuck! By the mid-19th century, a sparsely populated area, largely bypassed by the 18th century agricultural advances, became one of the most dynamic in Scotland. Road improvements and the coming of the railway provided a further boost.

Although later agricultural changes and ups-and-downs in the textile industry led to many people leaving in the 19th century, more came than left. However, the 20th century wars, a decline in demand for the products of the mills and the closure of the railway for 46 years, brought challenging times to the Leader and Gala Water valleys. After a bumpy ride through the second half of the 20th century, the area is back on the rails metaphorically, and, with the reopening of the Waverley railway line to Tweedbank in 2015, literally.

The story of Wedale and Lauderdale goes spinning on into the 21st century. We however follow the threads of past stories woven from the Wedale and Lauderdale landscape. We hear about a saintly boy called Malloch, a man with a tongue that could not lie and a woman who saved the day with a snowball in summer. We hear about some deathly Soor Plooms, meet a ghostly laird, and follow in the footsteps of pilgrims.

The Journey: 50 miles

From Tweedbank Station turn left at roundabout (signed Melrose), take second exit at next roundabout (signed Darnick/Gattonside) and turn first left onto B6374 (signed Gattonside).

Crossing the Tweed by the Bottle Brig, so called because its builders incorporated a bottle in the structure, we head towards Wedale. The

Southern Upland Way cuts across this road following an older route over the hills towards Lauder, but we continue alongside the Tweed and drop down into Elwyn Glen where the Allan or Elwyn Water emerges to join the river. Many a monk walked up the Elwyn to the Girthgate or Sanctuary Road to reach Soutra, the medieval hospital and hostel for devout travellers high on the Lammermuirs. On their way upstream travellers pass through the Fairy Dene or, as those too superstitious to name the fairy folk call it, the Nameless Dene. The local football team, Gala Fairydene Rovers, clearly had no such qualms!

Walter Scott is partly responsible for the ongoing association of the Elwyn Water with fairies: strange goings on up there feature in his novel *The Monastery*. There is however also the mysterious appearance from time to time of strangely shaped pieces of clay in the Fairydene. Local wisdom has it that they are fairy cups and plates. Some claim that vigorous swearing will persuade the Elwyn to deliver up a new set. However, heavy rainfall bringing a rush of water down the glen seems to be the prompt the fairies need to clear out their cupboards. A few of these fantastical shapes are displayed in the Museum of Scotland in Edinburgh. Whatever their origin, it is hard to believe they are made by any natural process.

Galashiels, straddling the Gala Water is one of the youngest towns in the Tweed valley. Although it was a late developer, the remains of ancient forts and towers in the hills around it are testimony to a lively past. Iron Age metal smelters plied their craft on the edge of the town, where in the mediaeval period men gathered for archery training at the 'bow butts'. After Normanised nobles superimposed the feudal system on Anglo Saxon arrangements, royal grants of land came with a formal obligation for landholders to provide men for military service. Archery practice was compulsory but James I, II, III and IV all had to issue decrees in the 15th century insisting on practice and banning the main distractions – golf and football – implying that few took this obligation seriously. The requirement to turn up for wappenschaws (weapon inspections) and archery practice lapsed after the Union of the Parliaments in 1707. Curiously, the law banning football was not repealed until 1907!

The land now occupied by the town was once part of the Royal Ettrick Forest, the very part that King Robert the Bruce granted to his faithful supporter the Good James Douglas in the early 14th century. At that time it was open woodland pasture for sheep and the 'shielings' (shelters) from which the town takes its name. From then on, the history and fortunes of Gala Water, Galashiels and its people were inextricably linked with the spinning of wool and the weaving and processing of woollen cloth. Although the Gala mills are gone, Heriot Watt University's School of Textiles and Design remains.

Following the signs to the town centre we come to halt alongside a magnificent statue of a mounted Border reiver, the work of Gala's own Thomas Clapperton. This, and the design of the Burgh Chambers behind it, hark back to the days of wappenshaws and it is to the heart of old Gala we now go.

Turn right then immediately left onto St Johns Street and, at T junction, left onto Scott Crescent.

Old Gala House on the left was built in 1457 by the Hoppringill family (later just Pringle) at a time when Gala was a cluster of cottages housing craftsmen and businesses catering for foresters and farmers. No castle and no abbey here! The Pringle family though were a powerful dynasty involved in the political affairs and intrigues of their day. Their empire at one time stretched as far north as this journey takes us and along the Tweed to Kelso.

A stone above the doorway of the original Old Gala House was carved with the following timeless advice from Elspeth, the wife of Robert Pringle:

Elspeth Dishington builted me
In sin lye not;
The things thou can'st not get,
Desyre not

In the usual practice of the time, she kept her father's name when she married. A later Pringle, James, was an innovator with an eccentric streak. He required his tenants to plant six cherry trees, or 12 other trees, or pay a fine. He also designed and funded the construction of a bridge over the Tweed to allow travellers from Melrose Abbey to access the Girthgate road to Soutra without getting their feet wet. It incorporated drawbridges to be raised in times of trouble, but the engineering skills of its designer were not, sadly, up to the job and this quirky bridge survived only in the place-name Bridgend.

The tragic drowning of 20 people on their way to Melrose Fair almost three centuries later illustrates why a bridge was needed. Competing accounts of what had caused the ferry to sink included allegations that hidden forces had been at work. A local woman claimed that she and the 'Evil One' had taken the form of 'twa corbies' (crows) and orchestrated the disaster from their position on the prow of the boat. The Kirk Session however recorded that it was one of 'several tokens of the Lord's anger evidenced against this place'. Conspiracy theories notwithstanding, most people probably accepted that the ferryman had made a fatal error – as it seems he had.

People being people though, as the town grew so did the stories of ghosts and other unnatural occurrences. As the tale of Tam Sanderson's night time visit to church suggests, Gala's residents were as superstitious as their rural neighbours.

Tam Sanderson's Rough Night

It was believed by some that the family burial vault of the Scotts, who by Sanderson's time were the lairds of Gala, opened up spontaneously for nine consecutive nights before the death of a family member. One night, Tom Sanderson the shoemaker, was having a few drinks in his local inn when he mentioned that he didn't hold with this superstitious stuff. Well, the reaction he got was predictable and before long he had accepted a dare to take the road through the kirkyard on his way home, enter the Kirk and, to prove he had been there, plant his shoemaker's awl in the floor of the laird's pew.

Off he went. His drinking buddies followed at a distance but stopped at the gate and watched as he staggered through the kirkyard and into the Kirk. There was a hushed silence among the men at the gate which was broken before long by piercing screams from inside the church. In they rushed to find Tom on the floor shouting that he was being held down by an evil spirit. Attempts to free him failed and, in the commotion that ensued, someone pulled the bell rope.

Summoned from their beds by the clanging of the church bell, folk ran towards the Kirk from all corners of the town. What terrible thing had happened? Was Gala under attack? Was the Gala Water about to flood the town? Speculation was rife. But, as the first of them reached the Kirk, they heard laughter from inside. Thinking it must be demonic laughter, many stopped in their tracks but a few brave souls carried on.

They were almost at the big oak doors when they burst open and out came a rowdy bunch of laughing men carrying Tom. He had passed out by this time, which was just as well because soon all the folk who had gathered were hooting with laughter too. When Tom's friends finally succeeded in freeing him from the grip of the terrible force that was pinning him to the ground, it became clear that, in his haste to drive the awl into the floor, he had driven it through his cobbler's apron, nailing himself to the floorboards.

There is no account of the aftermath but it is likely that all but Tom's pride soon recovered. As for the Scotts, they did not take the rumours that the vault could foretell the death of a family member too seriously – there was no watch on the vault that night.

By the time this story occurred, Galashiels was a Burgh of Barony with its own court. Handloom weavers from the town and surrounding area were bringing their cloth to one of several waulking or fulling mills to be processed and made ready for sale. The numbers of weavers living in the town waxed and waned between the 16th and 18th centuries. Some came to the area fleeing religious persecution elsewhere – Fleming is a common Border name – but others left due to religious persecution as, for example, when neighbour reported neighbour for being Covenanters in the 17th century, breaking up their looms or worse.

Beyond Old Gala House is the Market Cross. Here, at the heart of the old town, significant events in Gala's history are symbolically re-enacted during the annual Braw Lads Gathering. Among the events recalled is the story behind the 'Soor Plooms' that appear in the town's coat of arms. A group of local men surprised a party of English soldiers who were helping themselves to some sour plums in 1377, and killed them before they could attack the town.

The town song, though, celebrates not the town but the Braw, Braw Lads o' Gala Water with a rendering of an old ballad to which Robert Burns, who spent 26 days in the Borders when he was 29, put new words.

> *Braw, braw lads on Yarrow braes,*
> *They rove amang the blooming heather;*
> *But Yarrow braes, nor Ettrick shaws,*
> *Can match the lads o' Gala water.*

Fine as the Burns version is, a verse of the older lyrics deserves an airing:

> *Lothian lads are black wi' reek.*
> *And Teviotdale lads are little better;*
> *But she's kiltit her coats aboon her knee,*
> *And gane wi' the lad o' Gala Water.*

Leaving Gala's Braw Lad and Braw Lass behind, we drop down into the river valley.

Continue straight ahead to roundabout, turn left onto Albert Place (signed A7/ Town Centre) and take first left (a continuation of Albert Place).

Other than a corn mill, the earliest businesses here were waulking mills. Over the 19th century, however, first spinning and then weaving processes were mechanised and more mills sprang up beside the fast-flowing river. The move from hand spun to mill spun wool brought spinners in from the hills and changed the lives of many as these lines from a poem 'The Spinnin' O't', convey:

> But the folks now-a-days are a' turned sae braw,
> The laird an' the farmer, the cottar an' a',
> That the cairds are laid by, an' the wheel flung awa'.
> And mills maun be built for the spinnin' o't.

More mills crowded along the banks of Galawater when weaving was also mechanised, each staking a claim on the water needed to power their machinery. Such was the level of demand and the pressure on seasonally variable levels of water in the river that, from the late 1830s, mill owners were willing to invest in steam powered looms. The population of the town tripled from 2,000 in 1831 to 6,000 in 1851 (about the size of Selkirk now) and then tripled again to 18,000 by 1891. It was also a town with an increasingly diverse population. Mill owners and the workers who flocked to mills came with a wide range of faiths. One minister, Dr Douglas, took the wise view that 'while they are peaceable members of society and live soberly, righteously and godly, the speculative points on which they may differ are of little importance'.

The textile trade, although growing, was also subject to unpredictable downs. One enterprising Gala weaver, Robert Coulter, rode out the slumps of the weaving trade by making candy he sold in Melrose. His catchy advertising ditty, 'Coulter's Candy', became widely known across Scotland.

Allie Ballie, Allie Ballie Bee,
Sittin' on yer Mammie's knee,
Greetin' for a wee bawbee,
Tae buy some Coulter's Candy

Robert Coulter was fortunate to have something to fall back on in hard times. Many were not so lucky a century or so later, when Scotland's woollen textile industry began to struggle in the face of competition from man-made fabrics. One by one the Gala mills fell silent. Some upped their game to cater for the luxury market and kept going for a while but, unlike the mills in Selkirk and Hawick that still survive, eventually succumbed.

Before we move off again, a glance at the public library on the left is a reminder of the days when libraries were for paying members only. Sir Walter Scott was a member of Gala's subscription library and on one occasion sent a letter asking if the library held a copy of a recently published book. The response, penned by David Thomson, the chair and himself no mean poet, no doubt amused Scott:

We hae nae mony books in vogue,
As you'll see by the catalogue.
In truth, our funds are rather spare,
At present we can do nae mair,
We're ruined quite in oor finances
Wi' your bewitching, famed romances.

Leaving the Burgh Chambers, we follow the mounted reiver's gaze up stream.

Proceed along Bank Street and High Street to traffic lights and go straight ahead (signed A72 Peebles).

The road leaving the town runs through an area once busy with mills, then electronics factories and now retail outlets. Terraces of houses built to house mill workers line both sides of the valley. Despite three outbreaks of cholera in the town between 1843 and 1849, Galashiels did not get a piped water supply and therefore flushable toilets until 1915. Being the last town in the Borders to get piped water, Gala folk were the butt of jibes from residents of places better served – they called them 'Pail merks'. Mill owners and other wealthier townspeople meanwhile, for reasons we can guess at, had their houses built on hillsides overlooking the town or on its edge.

A comic tale of presumption and mistaken identity, committed to verse by Gala man Peter Coldwell, gives an insight into the consequences of Gala's increasing social segregation. This popular tale travelled far and was even translated into German.

Cuddy Peggy

Old Peggy was a hawker who travelled around selling needles, buttons and threads. Gala at this time had only one shop, affectionately known as 'Willie a' Things', so she did a good trade selling her wares around Gala and other burgeoning industrial towns on the Tweed. She was known as Cuddy Peggy because her wee packhorse cuddy Dauvit carried her stock in panniers.

One day though Dauvit fell sick.

> *And seein' him placed in this helpless condition,*
> *She thocht it her duty to get a physician.*
> *So away for that purpose she hastily set,*
> *When just on her way she the minister met.*

Peggy of course told the minister that Dauvit was unwell and she was off to fetch the doctor to which the minister replied:

> *'Indeed, to hear that I'm exceedingly sorry,*
> *But, if spared, I'll call down and see him to-morrow'*
> *So wi' that Margaret curtsied an' bade him good-bye,*
> *Syne away for the Doctor as fast's she could hie —*

Margaret found the doctor, who, happily, was able to diagnose and treat the poor beast successfully. The Minister, true to his word, came to find Margaret the next day. He was pleased to hear that Dauvit was better and, kind man that he was, offered to pray for him to which Margaret replied:

'The deil's in the man — wad ye pray for an ass?'
'O fie, Margaret, fie, why don't you think shame
To call your poor husband by any such name?'
'Ma husband! I daresay the minister's mad;
I've nae husband noo, tho at ae time I had'

The minister then asks if Dauvit is a relation of Margaret's – at which point she tells him he is her donkey.

'Oh, Margaret, I find that I've been mistaken,
I, David, your ass, for your husband have taken.
So pardon what I've in my ignorance said,
And the awkward mistake into which I've been led.'

So the parson nae langer protracted his stay.
But shook hands wi' auld Peggy, and bade her good-day.
And laughed a' the road hame till nearly distracted,
To think sic a part in the drama he'd acted.

Leaving Gala with laughter in our ears, the road follows the old coaching road along the left bank of the river.

Both banks of the Galawater were at one time thick with tower houses, most of them now wholly or partially ruined, or substantially modernised. Most belonged at one time or another to descendants of the Pringles. Old Buckholm Tower on Buckholm Hill on the other side of Gala Water was one of these. It was owned in the late 17th century by a James Pringle, whose exploits tarnished the otherwise generally good family name. He continued to haunt the tower and surrounding area after his death until he and those he terrified were spared further misery by a brave soul who figured out how to lift the curse.

The De'il o' Buckholm

James Pringle became known as The De'il o' Buckholm on account of his brutal treatment of those who crossed him. He made life as difficult as he could for neighbours he knew or suspected to be Covenanters.

In his official capacity as leader of the local militia, he led raids on Covenanter conventicles, and on one occasion returned to Buckholm Tower with two captives. One was an old man, Gibby Elliot, who fell as he was fleeing from the soldiers. The other was Gibby's son who stopped to help his father. Now, by rights the prisoners should have been taken to the Tolbooth in Galashiels but Pringle threw them in the dungeon of Buckholm Tower for the night.

During the evening, as he sat drinking by the fire, he remembered that a couple of centuries earlier a reiving band of Elliots and Armstrongs had killed his ancestor George when they attacked his tower at Torwoodlee. As he got drunker he got angrier until, eventually, he decided to interrogate the prisoners himself. His method of interrogation involved hanging his victims on hooks by their chins and, unsurprisingly, his captives died.

When Gibby's wife came to Buckholm Tower in the morning to find out what had befallen her menfolk, she learned they were dead, and left – but only after she had cursed the laird of Buckholm. Her curse was that he should be hounded as he had hounded her husband and son. And hounded he was. He spent the rest of his life tormented by the delusion that he was being chased by hounds. The sounds of his running feet and his screams continued to be heard in and around Buckholm Tower long after he died.

That is, until a local minister was brave enough to go into the house alone armed only with his Bible. He never spoke of what happened in there but the ghost of the De'il o' Buckholm and his tortured screams were gone for good.

Over on this side of the river, the road as we leave the town bends away from the river and in the land between sits Torwoodlee, the location for at least six historic buildings, each of which reflected the political conditions of its time.

Pass entrance to Torwoodlee (private road) and turn next right to park at top of hill for optional walk.

The oldest structure on this site was a Celtic British enclosure which may have been a gathering space. It was later overlaid with a Broch built after the Romans left, possibly for use as a command centre. Then came a peel tower which was destroyed in the attack on the Pringles that provoked the De'il of Buckholm to take revenge and, in its place was built a now ruined 17th century tower house. This was finally replaced by a late 18th century country mansion, Torwoodlee House, built for comfort and to impress.

And, beneath these layers there are several underground bunkers. They were created during World War II for use in the event that the UK was occupied by the Nazis. They were to be secret intelligence centres, fitted out with state of the art communications systems of the day. Local milkmen and postmen, the eyes and ears of the town, were trained to gather intelligence and report to these centres if the worst should happen. Neither the bunkers nor Torwoodlee House are open to the public, but the earlier broch and tower are accessible on foot from the car park.

Torwoodlee Broch may have been linked in some way to a smaller broch upriver on the other side near Bow Castle. These are two of only three enigmatic and mysterious brochs in the Scottish Borders. Who built them? And why is this still the subject of speculation? Most brochs are in areas which were known to be controlled by the Picts, and these ones are ideally positioned to dominate the mid-Tweed area with its routes north and south. Did the Picts take over from the Romans as nominal overlords of the Selgovae, the local native British population, but allow them to carry on their day to day lives with little interference? We don't know but after it had served its purpose, or even while the Picts were here, Torwodlee Broch was occupied by the Celtic British.

Soutra Aisle

The purpose of the Catrail, a section of which runs between the broch and the road, is also a mystery. It is a substantial earthwork running south from Torwoodlee through Teviotdale to the modern border with England. Also created after the Romans left, it was unlikely to have been defensive. For one thing, there are big gaps between sections which prompted writer Herbert Maxwell to quip: 'If [defence] was the origin and purpose of the Catrail, it is to be hoped that the Britons were better Christians than they were military engineers'. The Catrail may have marked a boundary between lands held by different groups – a symbolic rather than a military border. This was the edge of the hilly Selgovae country, and perhaps this tribe needed the Picts as allies to maintain the balance of power in the area. With other Celtic British tribes to the east and north and the Scots to the west, such an alliance would make sense.

Return to A72, turn right and proceed to Clovenfords.

Clovenfords was for many centuries an important gateway to the west towards Peebles, north towards Edinburgh, and south to where, before the late 18th century road improvements, the Tweed was fordable. It served as a transport interchange and, until the 19th century, was bigger than both Galashiels and Innerleithen. The Edinburgh to Carlisle stagecoach, the bus service of its day, stopped at the Inn to rest horses, drop off, pick up and often feed passengers along with those who came to collect or see them off. It also delivered and collected mail, a role later taken over by trains. Trains also picked up the six tons of grapes grown annually by the enterprising William Thomson, and dropped off supplies of coal for the water heating system that kept his hothouses at the right temperature. Grapes from Tweed Vineyards found their way onto tables in restaurants and homes of those wealthy enough to buy them from fruit markets the length and breadth of Britain – until air travel opened this market to imported grapes grown more cheaply in sunnier climates.

At roundabout take B710 exit (signed Bowland).

Following the stage coach route over the rolling hills we are still in historic Pringle territory. Hidden in the hills are several of their erstwhile towers. Some are now beyond repair but some like Whytbank Tower have been restored, or like Bowland, now a country house set in a designed landscape, were modernised and are in private hands.

At T junction turn left onto A7 (signed Edinburgh).

Crossing the river and passing the sites of Bow Castle and the remains of the broch mentioned earlier up on the hill, we travel to Stow, or to give it its proper name, Stow in Wedale. This place has long been important to Christian pilgrims. Indeed, Stow means a holy place. Its status as such is associated with St Mary's or Our Lady's Well just south of Stow at Torsonce Wood. It is thought that Arthur drank from this well after the 7th century Battle of Wedale, and later expressed his gratitude for the victorious outcome by founding a chapel nearby.

In mediaeval times Stow was an important place of sanctuary. As long as perpetrators of crime stayed within a designated area, the girth, they could not be arrested – and the Wedale or Stow girth covered the whole parish. A section of the hill road from the Eildons to Soutra is called Girthgate and probably marks the boundary of the Wedale girth. Churches themselves were often places of sanctuary. Breaking the King's peace by apprehending someone who had taken refuge in the church was punishable by fines. Churches and girths were though only temporary refuges. Lawbreakers had to answer for their crimes in the king's courts or go into hiding as outlaws – as Robert the Bruce did in the early 14th century after he murdered his rival the Red Comyn in a church. Whether he killed him by intent, accident or in self-defence was irrelevant – 'murdrum' was murdrum!

The buildings in Stow, notably the churches and the Bishops Palace, reflected its special status in the diocese of St Andrews. A mid-13th century church, also dedicated to St Mary and rebuilt in the 14th century, became the Old Kirk when the newer and grander church that superseded it took the St Mary's name. The size of the church and its soaring spire were a statement of the wealth of its patrons and, of local pride in Stow's status. Pilgrims also came to see a large boulder said to bear the imprint of the Virgin Mary's foot until it mysteriously disappeared. The work of the fairies? Or of workmen on road repairs unaware that it was no ordinary stone?

Across the road from St Mary's Church, there is the incongruous sight of an old bridge leading nowhere. This was a packhorse bridge, built in 1655 to connect the village with the road, then on the other side of the river. Now the good folk of Stow could climb aboard a coach to Edinburgh of Galashiels with dry feet. Until the turnpike roads were built, stretches of this road were in such a poor state that carts, coaches and horses often preferred to take their chances in the river bed.

As we head north we pass through an area once thick with Iron Age enclosures and Roman fortlets. The fort at Gilston, where we leave the Galawater to cut across the hills to the Leader Water, was one of the latter.

At junction with B6368 turn right (signed Soutra Aisle).

The road across the hills follows a route that for millennia was an informal boundary between what is now the Scottish Borders and the Lothians. A signpost marks where the Roman road Dere Street, later called the Via Regia or Royal Road, cuts across our road. This route also marks the outer boundary of an area that was at one time covered in buildings associated with Soutra, the medieval hospital. Visitors were rewarded, then as now, with a magnificent panoramic view encompassing the Pentland Hills, Edinburgh, the Firth of Forth, East Lothian and the North Sea. Soutra – 'the farm with the wide view' – is aptly named!

The solitary building at the side of the road is a burial vault for the acquisitive Pringle family. Nothing remains of the hospital founded by King Malcolm IV of Scotland in the 12th century. It was already offering hospitality to travellers (the original meaning of 'hospitium'), succour to the poor and medical services to the sick and infirm. Later Soutra gained an international reputation and became the largest and wealthiest hospital in Scotland. Archaeological and written evidence of surgical and medical procedures, and of the herbs used to treat patients and manage pain, reveals how skilled the monks were. As the information boards here explain, many of the plants grown were, in the wrong hands, capable of taking rather than saving life.

In the 1460s however, the misdemeanours of Prior Stephen Fleming resulted in him being stripped of office by the Pope. Details of what Stephen did to merit this are buried deep in the archives of the Vatican but, whatever his transgression, it was the beginning of the end for Soutra. The King transferred management of the hospital to Trinity College Church in Edinburgh and confiscated its vast landholdings. This land had generated income to keep the hospital going and although Soutra survived the Reformation, it finally closed its doors in the 1650s.

Proceed to A68 junction and turn right (signed Jedburgh).

The A68, running parallel with Roman Dere Street and the medieval Girthgate, climbs into a forest of elegant wind turbines then drops to follow the Leader Water down to the Tweed. This part of Lauderdale is rich in incident and story, accompanying the long scenic descent to Lauder.

St Cuthbert

One night, in the year 651, a young man called Malloch was tending his family's sheep in these hills when he had a vision of a soul ascending to heaven, like a shooting star. When he returned home and told his family what he had seen, they told him that the Abbot of the abbey at Old Melrose had died the very same night.

Surely, thought Malloch, it was Abbot Aidan's soul he saw ascending to heaven, and it was a sign for him to become a monk. So he took his leave of the family and went off with his horse and spear to the abbey to report his vision and offer himself as a novice. Prior Boisil welcomed the young man and gave him his monk's name – Cuthbert. When Abbot Boisil died of plague ten years later, Cuthbert succeeded him as the Abbot of Melrose Abbey and later became Abbot at Lindisfarne.

Young Malloch may or may not have been born in upper Lauderdale, but he did shepherd here. A well from which Cuthbert drank sits by Dere Street. It was later dedicated to him and a church built at Channelkirk.

The Borderers of Cuthbert's time were subjects of the Kingdom of Northumbria. A few decades before he was born, a battle took place down the road at Addingston, just beyond Carfraemill, which was to shape Cuthbert's destiny and that of his neighbours. The Battle of Degaston was won by the Angles who later captured Edinburgh, so gaining control of all lands to the south of it. This is why Cuthbert's career took him from the Abbey of Old Melrose, to Ripon, now in Yorkshire, and later to Lindisfarne, in Northumberland, both now on the English side of the border.

Although it had no abbey of its own, the abbeys were of immense importance to Lauderdale. Their sheep grazed in thousands on the hills, watched over by shepherds to guard them from predators. After the

Reformation people lived here much as they had done before, only now they paid rent to a laird for the privilege of having land to farm.

One such farm, rented from the Earl of Lauderdale, sat high in hills above Carfraemill. Here at one time lived a woman known as Midside Maggie whose quick wits saved the day not once, but twice.

The Snowball and the Bannock

When Thomas Hardie married Maggie Lylestone and took her to live on his hillside farm at Midside on Tollis Hill, he knew he had married a resourceful woman. But little did he know how resourceful she would turn out to be!

Together they planted and tended their kailyard, and the sheep that roamed the hills. Things went well until there was a run of bad winters and springs. Many of their sheep and lambs died and, as meat from the lambs and the wool from the sheep was their only source of income, they fell on hard times.

The day came that Maggie had to go to Lauder and tell the laird that they had no money to pay the rent. Now the laird was none too popular with his tenants, but he liked Maggie so he said, 'I tell you what, I'll half the rent for Midside for the year if you give me a kiss.' Maggie's response was instant – and it was 'No!' She knew where that kiss would lead and besides, she did not even have enough money for half the rent.

Although she had rebuffed him and the laird was not one to do his tenants any favours, he secretly admired Maggie's bravery and said gruffly, 'Well, if there's that much snow on Tollis Hill in the winter, bring me a snowball as rent next June'. Sure that he had set her an impossible challenge, he added, 'If you bring me a snowball, not only will that pay next year's rent for Midside but I'll wipe the slate clean of your rent arrears.'

Back went Maggie to Midside to tell her husband about the deal she had struck. He was proud of her ability to stand her ground against the laird and strike a deal, but secretly he must have had doubts. Even if Maggie could somehow produce a snowball in June, would the laird honour his part of the bargain? Maggie however, had faith. And a plan. One day, when the land lay under a thick blanket of snow, she climbed the hill, searched out a cleft in the rock that the sun's rays never reached, and packed it with handful after handful of snow. Then she sealed the cleft with moss and went home.

When June and the next rent day came around, Maggie went to collect her snowball. Beneath the plug of moss there was the snow, as white as the day she put it there. She pulled out a big lump, wrapped it in a blanket to keep it cool and set off towards Lauder as fast as she could. When she presented the snowball to the laird, he sighed and said, 'Well, a promise is a promise. You owe me nothing for arrears and Midside is yours rent free for another year.'

A few years later Maggie's ingenuity saved the life of the very man she had refused to kiss! He had by now inherited the grand title of Earl of Lauderdale, but things had not gone well for him. The Earl, a Royalist, found himself on the losing side at the Battle of Worcester in 1651. He was taken prisoner and thrown in the dungeons of the Tower of London where he languished for several years.

When the Earl didn't return and Maggie heard that things were looking pretty bad for him, she came up with a plan. He had after all honoured his promise to accept a snowball in summer as rent, and had written off their arrears so saving them from poverty and starvation. Perhaps she thought, the rent money they had saved up to give him on his return would be enough to buy his freedom. But how would she get it to him?

In those days, prisoners relied on visitors to bring them food. So Maggie baked the gold coins saved for rent into a bannock and set off dressed as a boy to deliver it. When she arrived at the Tower she wandered around singing an old ballad about the Leader Haughs to a tune she knew the Earl would recognise.

Weak as he was, he heard the song and called for his guards to let the singer visit him in his cell. They searched Maggie but somehow failed to notice that she was no boy but a grown woman. Nor did they spot that the bannock weighed a great deal more than a bannock should. Perhaps, being the clever woman she was, she had kept a coin or two aside to buy their silence. We'll never know, but we do know that she delivered the bannock and shortly after, the Earl was released from the Tower of London. With the money Maggie had brought he escaped to Holland. And there he stayed until Charles regained his throne in 1660 and it was safe to come back.

Lest anyone think this is an unlikely story, the silver girdle the Earl of Lauderdale gave Maggie as a reward was gifted by her descendants to the Museum of Scotland in Edinburgh. The snowball she paid him as rent melted long ago.

Lauder started life as a moorland frontier town located between where it is now and Dere Street, or as it was later called, Malcolm's Road, the Via Regia or King's Road. It relocated to a site near the castle, or rather, castles. The current Thirlestane Castle, situated on the southern edge of the town, replaced and incorporated bits of a previous castle, which was itself built inside a medieval fort, which was itself built on or close to a Celtic British stronghold.

One of Lauder's older castles features in 'The Ballad of Auld Maitland' which first appeared in written form in Walter Scott's *Minstrelsy of the Scottish Borders*. He heard it from James Hogg who got it from his mother Margaret Laidlaw, who had it from her grandfather who heard it from... This lengthy poem, like many Border ballads, is partly dramatic fiction. It refers to Edward I's attack on Lauder Castle in 1296. The English troops:

> ... far'd up o'er Lammermor
> They burn'd baith tower and town
> Until they came to a derksome house,
> Some call it Leaders Town
> Whae hauds this house young Edward cries,
> Or whae gae'st ower to me?
> A grey-haired knight set up his head
> And cracked right crousely
> Of Scotland's King I haud my house
> He pays me meat and fee
> And I will keep my guid auld house
> While my house will keep me.

Auld Maitland successfully defended the castle on this occasion, but the Borders as a whole paid a heavy price for resisting Edward I. His troops massacred those who opposed them and burned towns, crops and houses, carrying off, so they claimed, 15 shiploads of plunder. According to the ballad, Auld Maitland's three sons who were serving with Edward in France, espied a standard captured at Lauder. They then avenged the attack on Thirlestane, ignoring chivalric decorum in favour of the Borderers' 'eye for an eye' code.

The Maitlands, who took the title of Earls of Lauderdale, were for many centuries at the heart of Scottish politics and intellectual life. William Maitland who was nicknamed Meikle Wylie (a play on Machiavelli – he had a reputation for political manoeuvrings) was Mary Queen of Scots' Secretary of State. A loyal servant, he may have been involved in the plot to murder Mary's husband Darnley but he paid for his loyalty with his life in 1573. That event echoes another which took place in Lauder in 1482, when a showdown between King James III's advisers and a group of disaffected nobles culminated in the king being forced to witness six of his favourite courtiers hung from Lauder Bridge.

Belling the Cat

James III surrounded himself with learned men, musicians and craftsmen. He enjoyed their company but also relied on their advice to promote the revival of learning and the arts and other features of the Italian Renaissance he admired. The landowning nobles were not at all impressed. For one thing, they had less influence with the king than they believed they were entitled to. Their resentment had been simmering for some time.

An earlier plot to get rid of the King's favourites had been foiled and the ringleaders imprisoned in Craigmillar Castle near Edinburgh. One of them died but the other, Albany, escaped and fled to France. So determined was Albany to bring down James III, that he offered his support to the Duke of Gloucester (later Richard III of England) to invade Scotland. He of course wasn't going to turn down an offer like that and English troops were duly sent north in 1482.

When James III heard that an English army had reached the border and had already captured Berwick upon Tweed, he summoned his Scottish nobles to meet him and his advisers in Lauder church. The nobles, led by the enormously powerful Archibald Douglas, Earl of Angus, got there first. While they waited for the king they talked tactics and agreed that they should refuse to support the king until he got rid of his inner circle of 'fiddlers and bricklayers'. But who was going to be their spokesperson? Archibald Douglas, likening the nobles to mice with a common interest in outwitting a cat, spoke up and said 'I will bell the cat'.

When the King and his advisers arrived, Douglas ushered them into the church. As they filed in, Douglas stepped forward as if to greet Cochrane, the King's particular favourite. Instead, he tore the gold chain from his neck, saying a rope would suit him better. The king and his advisers were trapped. The nobles then subjected them to a mock trial. Finding all but one of the advisors guilty, they dragged them from the church and, before a powerless and horrified James III, hung them from the parapet of the bridge. They showed mercy to only one, Ramsey, who was spared on grounds of youth.

Neither the bridge nor the church has survived, but that particular Earl of Angus went down in history as Archibald 'Bell the Cat' Douglas.

Leave Lauder and proceed to Earlston.

A few miles downstream is Earlston. This was the only place of any size on this side of the Tweed valley when the abbeys were founded. Unlike Lauder, it never became a Royal Burgh, but it was here that David 1 came in 1136 to sign the charter founding Melrose Abbey. The Earls of March had their principal castle here, from which they controlled Lauderdale, Lammermuir and lands to the east. Although it was quickly eclipsed by Galashiels, Earlston produced significant quantities of gingham, linen and woollen textiles in the 18th and early 19th centuries. And until the coming of the railways, Earlston was an important market town for the local black cattle and horses and, from the 18th century, held three hiring fairs a year. There, farmers recruited agricultural labour for the season, bought and sold animals and supplies, and frequented local hostelries.

Earlston is however best known as the home of Thomas Learmont, more familiar as Thomas the Rhymer or True Thomas.

Thomas the Rhymer

Thomas was born in the early 13th century into the family who owned Learmonth Tower and lands along the river Leader. He was employed in his youth as bard to the Earls of March, travelling around with them entertaining high born audiences with stories in song or verse. He became an accomplished linguist – he spoke English and Old Welsh and read Latin. He was also the first Scottish poet to write in English, albeit Scots English. Said to be the author of 'Sir Tristem', a retelling of the Tristram and Isolde story, some, including Sir Walter Scott, considered him the father of Scottish poetry.

Thomas though is best remembered not for his linguistic prowess or skill as a writer, but as a seer. Such was belief in the accuracy of his prophecies that they were consulted before important decisions were made, as for example before the Jacobite rebellions of 1715 and 1745. Thomas was not however born with the ability to foretell the future. He claimed that he was granted his powers of prophecy by the Queen of the Fairies, after he had spent seven years in her kingdom.

Thomas's meeting with the Queen of the Fairies was recounted in Journey 1, when we visited Huntlybank on the slopes of the Eildons. However, another Huntlybank may have better claim to be the true location. This Huntlybank lies north east of Earlston near Corsbie Tower in the Lammermuirs behind Brotherstone, and is much more accessible from Ercildoune. To get to the Eildons, Thomas would have had to row himself across the river or find a safe place to ford, which is hardly the plan of a man just out for a daunder!

Wherever they met and whether he was, as he claimed, in Elfland for seven years; or on a gap year that lasted for seven; or living in secret with an earthly woman in another part of Scotland; or off being a spy, he did return to Earlston. And when he did he had a tongue that could not lie and the gift of prophecy. This he explained was granted as he was leaving, when the Queen of the Fairies made him promise never to speak of what he had seen in the fairy kingdom. She rewarded him for his service to her with an apple;

> *'take this for your wages Thomas,*
> *it will give you a tongue that can never lee'*

Thomas kept his promise to the Fairy Queen to return to Elfland if she called him, as she did by sending two while deer to fetch him some years later. Some believe he did return to the fairy kingdom and will return again. Others think he may have been assassinated. Others still believe that he went into seclusion at the hospital at Soutra.

Many before Thomas had seen visions – Cuthbert, Drythelm, Boisil – but they were holy visions and these men lived apart from the lay community. Is it a coincidence that, like Michael Scot who also had extraordinary skills and knowledge, Thomas was absent from the Borders for long periods of time? Perhaps, though, the responsibilities of lairdship and fame as a prophet simply weighed too heavily. A charter recording that his son had transferred the family lands to Soutra hospital, might suggest that is where he went... but then again, perhaps he lives still with the Queen of the Fairies.

Whatever the truth about Thomas, a ballad telling of his meeting with the Queen of the Fairies began to circulate barely a century after his death. His prophesies are mentioned in English and French manuscripts and became even more widely known after the invention of the printing press. Collections of his poems and prophecies sold all over Scotland from early 17th century and have influenced writers, including his 19th century Russian blood relative Mikhail Lermontov, ever since.

As for his prophecies, John Geddie, who collected Rhymer lore, commented that True Thomas's sayings 'cling to this countryside like burrs to a beggar's rags'. There were a lot of them! Some are mentioned in our other journeys, but one related specifically to Earlston: as long as a certain thorn tree stood, he said, 'Ercildoune shall possess all her lands'. In 1814, the tree was felled and shortly afterwards, Earlston sold off its common lands to settle debts. In case we are tempted to dismiss Thomas's prophecies, or put those which seem to have been fulfilled down to coincidence, it is worth remembering that he also said:

When the saut gaes abune the meal,
Believe nae mair in Thomas's tale.

As salt still costs less than flour perhaps we should give him the benefit of the doubt. And, if that is the case, there is one prophecy that may yet come true:

York was, London is, Edinburgh will be
The biggest o' the three.

Thomas's home, Rhymer's Tower, is now a ruin, but was still standing in the early 19th century when a certain Patrick Murray lived there. Sir Walter Scott gave the impression that there was something of the wizard about him too. He described Murray as a herbalist with a musical clock, an electrical machine and a stuffed alligator. In fact, as Robert Chambers later wrote, poor Patrick was a respected doctor who happened to have a collection of exotic objects and an interest in philosophy, science and self-invented gadgets. These included, in addition to those Walter Scott noted, a weather cock connected mechanically to his office and a barometer which enabled him to predict the weather without going outside. That may well have set local tongues wagging. Robert Chambers added 'that when the latest and most enlightened so strangely distort and mystify the character of a philosophical surgeon, can we doubt that 500 years have played still stronger tricks with the history and character of Thomas the Rhymer?'

South of Earlston is the White Hill famed for the yellow flowers of the broom immortalised in a well-known ballad 'The Broom o' the Cowdenknowes'.

Broom of the Cowdenknowes

The ballad can be traced back to the early 17th century when it was said that the covering of broom on the hill was so lush that a horseman could ride through it unseen – ideal conditions for secret trysts. Cowdenknowes at the foot was the site of just such a tryst.

Bonnie Mary to the ewe-bughts is gane
To milk her Daddy's ewes,
And yet as she sang, her sweet voice it rang
Right over the tops o' the nows.

The story has parallels with Tamlane in that a passing man seduces a local girl out on her own. In this ballad, the girl thinks she recognises the man as the son of a local laird but he denies it. Before he leaves, however, he gives her money and promises to return. When he passes that way again a few months later with some friends, he sees that she is visibly pregnant and insists, despite her protestations, that she had 'a gude man at home', and that the baby is the result of their tumble in the broom.

He's taen her by the waist sae sma
And he's set her on ahin'
Says, 'your father can ca his kye when he likes,
But ye'll never ca them out again.

I am the laird o the Youghal Tree Wells,
I hae thirty plows and three;
An' I hae gotten the bonniest lass
that's in a' the south countrie'

A happy ending to a border ballad at last! That said, later versions of the ballad tell the story from the girl's point of view and add that she misses home and longs for 'the bonnie broom'.

Sitting just to the south of the White Hill, is the Black Hill on top of which there was once a Celtic British enclosure. This probably belonged to the Votadini, neighbours to the Selgovae, who constructed the enclosure on top of Eildon Hill North just across the Tweed. Little is known about the relationship between the two tribes but we do know that the Black Hill later had a black reputation to match its name. The sometime laird of an estate at the foot of this hill was known locally not just for his harsh treatment of people who crossed him, but for personally dispatching those he felt merited the ultimate punishment –

hanging them or rolling them down the Black Hill in barrels full of nails.

Passing Drygrange, once a granary for Melrose Abbey, we follow the Leader to its journey's end. The Leader has inspired many to verse, including Norman McCaig who, being a keen fisherman, found this an evocative place:

By Leader Water

Behind my back, in the quietest hush of night,
An old ewe coughed. All that I think of men
Raised my hair up then stroked it down again.

And, on this note, we leave Lauderdale.

Turn left before Leaderfoot bridge (signed Kelso) and, at junction with the B6360, turn right (signed Galashiels).

Passing below two of Leaderfoot's three bridges, we follow the road the Romans built along the north bank of the Tweed to link Trimontium on the other bank to their fort at Lyne further up the Tweed. Approaching Gattonside, we enter Melrose Abbey's larder. The orchards on the sunny south facing slopes supplied the monks with fruit while honey from hillside beehives and some of the abbey's grain was stored here. Gattonside House was built in the early 19th century for Adam Ferguson, a leading figure in the Scottish Enlightenment. With his strong belief in the social importance of community, he would no doubt approve that today it is a care home with strong links to the community.

At T junction with the B6374 turn left to cross the Tweed and follow signs to Tweedbank Station.

Journey 5

Kelso and Yetholm

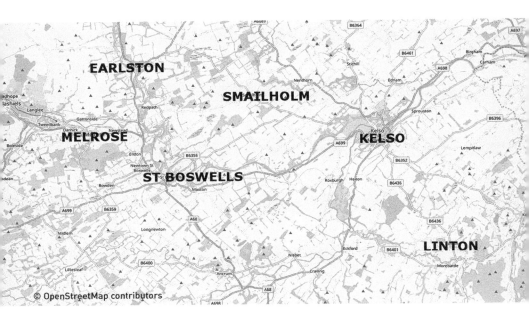

We travel now towards what was a historically fluid border. The Tweed winds eastward through red sandstone rocks with, on the north side, volcanic ridges and outcrops and, on the south side, a low-lying flood plain. This land has been peopled for at least 6,000 years. Two millennia ago the Celtic British Votadini lived here. By chance, or perhaps design, the Romans routed Dere Street along the boundary between them and their neighbours, the Selgovae. There are Roman camps and fortlets along this route and along the Cheviot Hills, but otherwise the echo of Roman footsteps here is faint.

The Romans were long gone when the Angles engulfed the Celtic British territories of northern England and south east Scotland to create the Kingdom of Northumbria. Anglo Saxon influence was particularly strong here and in neighbouring Teviotdale. This was due to geography but also because the area was colonised earlier and for longer than the lands to the north. Villages built around a central green appeared, and 'Ynglis' replaced Cymric as the main language. The abbeys and priories established to spread the Christian message were satellites of Lindisfarne far to the south. After a few generations of spiritual and secular rule from the other side of the Cheviots, the people here no doubt thought of themselves as Northumbrian.

But change was coming. Pressed by the Vikings from the south and Scots from the north, the Kingdom of Northumbria began to disintegrate. During the 11th century the Scots gained control of the area north of Leaderfoot. Then in the 12th century, Normans infiltrated Scotland by means of a royal marriage rather than force; the social, economic and cultural changes they brought had long lasting consequences.

Scotland's first Scoto-Norman king, David I, was religious and a superb strategist. As the Earl of Northumberland, he established a regional command centre at Roxburgh Castle. The four abbeys he later founded stimulated economic activity which was tapped and further boosted by his burghs. The trading privileges he granted the burghs connected local to regional markets and, in the case of royal burghs, to national and international markets. Wool produced by the vast flocks the abbeys owned was channelled through Roxburgh to Berwick-upon-Tweed and shipped off to European markets.

The strategic and economic importance of Roxburgh was though a mixed blessing. First to come under attack and last to be free of retreating armies, the area suffered greatly from national struggles for control of Scotland and its borders. These rumbled on for centuries and a great deal of blood was spilled. Whoever occupied the castle and the town had political and economic control of the lower Tweed all the way to Berwick-upon-Tweed and the North Sea trade routes. Sometimes people were subjects of an English king, sometimes of a Scottish one.

Much blood was also spilled in family feuding, cross border raids and disputes that had nothing to do with national struggles. The Laws of the Marches were put in place in the 13th century to deal with crimes and disputes involving parties from opposite sides of the border. Each of the three Marches (East, Middle and West) had two wardens: one responsible for the Scottish side and the other for the English. Cases were dealt with at designated places on March truce days, so called because, other than those on trial, everyone else was immune from prosecution. March Law became redundant after 1603 but the term 'march', meaning a boundary, remained in use. Burgh officials rode around the perimeter of the common lands annually to check that local farmers had not encroached on any land. Much of the common land later passed into private hands, but the ceremonial riding of the marches remains a central feature of the annual Common Ridings in the Border towns.

In more settled conditions after the Union of Parliaments in 1707, landowners and farmers turned to exploiting the area's richest natural resource – its land. This area was at the heart of a revolution in agriculture which paved the way for the industrial revolution. The 1695 Run Rig law had legalised the enclosure of land and removed barriers to terminating tenancies in order to create bigger farms. It was not long before the farmers of the Merse became pioneers of agricultural innovation. They drained land to bring more ground into cultivation, fertilised it to improve yields, introduced new crops and rotations, while acquiring and inventing new equipment. The result was a much more regulated landscape which poets such as George Henderson of Chirnside lamented:

Our bonny burnsides they hae drained and dug,
The crooks o' the burn they hae altered too;
The green ferny knowes where the hare lay snug,
They hae cleared o' ilk buss, and riven wi' the pleugh.
The bonny green braes by the foggy dell
Where grew the broom and the black slae thorn,
They hae levelled down wi' a purpose fell,
And Nature laments aa her beauties torn.

These changes did however result in Roxburghshire's farmland feeding greater numbers of people than before – but at a cost. Fewer workers were needed to farm the land and the terms on which agricultural labour was employed changed. These were the days of hiring fairs. Men, the hinds, were hired for six months or perhaps a year. In return for a wage and a roof over their head, they contracted to do heavy work, in particular ploughing. In George Douglas' evocation of 'The Border Ploughman':

Jock Tamson is the ploughman's name,
He dwalls on Scotlan's Border;
Frae stable-heck tae reddin-kaim
His gear is aye in order.
He drives twa horses o' the best,
An' few like him can guide them–
I doot there's nane wad stand the test
To draw a fur' (row) beside them.

The hind was also contracted to provide the services of a bondager, a woman to do lighter work like sow seed, milk cows and bring in the harvest. She might be the hind's wife or daughter, or a young woman the hind took on and paid from his own wages. But as Jack Hay perceptively observed in the early 20th century:

It's the Bondager who works the most, if I'm allowed to say
My word they fairly cop it on a busy threshing day;
They cairry strae tae yonder, tae the stable and the byre,
And up a twenty-five fit ladder, and very often higher.

The bondage system suited farmers but had obvious disadvantages for hinds and bondagers, not least that each time they were hired by a new employer they had to move. By the early 20th century the system was on the way out, as further labour saving technologies reduced seasonal demand for labour, and farmers began to employ workers on longer contracts.

Many however were unable to find farm work and were forced to leave the area in a process later dubbed the Lowland Clearances. Hand-spinning and hand-weaving of linen and woollen cloth provided employment for some in the 18th century, but these trades declined as one by one textile processes were mechanised in the 19th century. Some villages and small towns which had survived the destruction of war and rampaging armies in the 16th and 17th centuries (some did not), shrank or disappeared over the next two centuries as people left and larger farms provided for the needs of their horses and labourers themselves. Villages fortunate enough to have an inn and the passing trade of travellers fared a little better.

This history explains why attempts to erode what little control people had over their lives met with fierce resistance. This was especially so in religion. There was strong Covenanting resistance here to royal imposition of Church of England ways on Scotland's Presbyterian churchgoers in the 17th century. A century later, this area was one of the earliest to protest about the Act of Patronage which denied parishioners a say in the choice of a minister. And churchgoers here were at the forefront of a series of subsequent splits from and within the Church of

Scotland. John Wesley, founder of the Methodist church, recognised fertile recruiting ground when he accepted an invitation to preach in Kelso in the 1770s.

Stories abound of heroism, cleverness, ghosts and witches in the area many poems about topics as diverse as bridges, rural life, social protest and love in all its forms. There are though fewer tales of encounters with fairy folk than elsewhere in the Borders. On this journey, we visit an invisible castle and a ghost town, and meet cattle that could scale walls, a knight who slew a giant worm, Gypsy royalty, and a dastardly laird who met his just desserts.

The Journey: 60–65 miles

From Tweedbank Station turn left at roundabout (signed Melrose), follow signs for A68 North (signed Edinburgh) cross Tweed at Leaderfoot and take first right (signed Kelso) then left at T junction (signed Smailholm).

Passing Brotherstone farm, there are traces on the hill beyond (not visible from the road) of ancient cultivation terraces and a trio of standing stones – the two Brother stones, and below them, the Cow Stone. What these stones meant to the people who erected and visited them is unclear, but they are aligned with a henge at Mellerstain to the east, and were perhaps part of a grander design linking stones, people and the universe. An ancient circular stone structure at Whitrighill to the right of the road may also have been part of this complex, but whatever its function, the Romans showed no respect, raiding the stones to build Dere Street.

This place would have been known to Cuthbert, or young Malloch whom we met in Lauderdale. A degree of mystery shrouds his early life but he seems to have lived for a time with his foster mother, Kenspid, at a place called Hrungingham or Wrangholm, a long gone settlement between Brotherstone and Smailholm. Having a foster mother did not mean he had been orphaned. It was common for families of all ranks to 'lend' older children to members of their extended family who needed protection or help with tasks. Although Channelkirk in the Lammermuirs has a strong claim to be where Malloch saw Aidan's soul ascending to heaven 'with the sight of his spiritual eyes', it may have been here, closer to Old Mailros, that he had his vision.

Sir Walter Scott also knew this landscape and its stories well. He spent some of his young life at his grandparent's farmhouse at Sandyknowe in the shadow of Smailholm Tower and went to church in the village.

Enter Smailholm and park beside church.

A Childhood Gift

Smailholm's 17th century church incorporates elements of its 12th century predecessor. The two stained windows dedicated to St Giles and St Cuthbert were installed in 1907 to commemorate Sir Walter Scott. A local minister, W. J. Sime, is credited with spreading the idea that Wrangholm was where St Cuthbert had his vision. He was certainly media savvy and would now be described as a blogger. His stream of anonymous letters to the Scotsman newspaper, between 1909 and 1933, reported notable weather and natural events. He later published these letters as 'Nature Letters Book', dedicated it to 'the children of Smailholm Parish in their Generation', and gifted a copy to every child in the parish.

Sime writes, 'it is astonishing how religious cults survive until we have forgotten their meaning... to this day there are hosts of folk, including the writer, who eagerly hail the new moon with three bows in salute.' One of this book's authors has continued a family tradition of having southernwood in her garden without knowing the origin of the practice – until she read the copy of 'Nature Letters Book' which Mr Sime put in the hand of her father, a child of Smailholm. Pieces of sweet smelling 'suthrenwood', a plant associated with St Ninian the early Christian missionary, were commonly placed in family Bibles. Mr Sime does not however explain why. Was it to venerate St Ninian? Or simply to keep the Bible free of bookworms? Southernwood is a form of wormwood widely used in folk medicine.

How many other things do we unthinkingly do which connect us invisibly to distant ancestors?

Turn around, turn left at sign for Smailholm Tower and proceed through the farmyard of Sandyknowe Farm to Tower.

Perched on Sandyknowe Crags, Smailholm Tower was built in the 15th century by the Pringles who owned much land in Wedale and Lauderdale. It later passed to the even more powerful Scotts of Harden who had lands and towers in Teviotdale, Ettrick, Yarrow and Lauderdale. With its panoramic view south across the upper end of the Merse to the Cheviot Hills and down the Teviot valley, west to Ettrick, and, from the very top of the tower, to Bamburgh Castle on the Northumberland coast, this tower was quite a prize! It was also pretty well impregnable. Then, as now, the tower could only be accessed by clambering up a rocky path.

With its reed-fringed lochan at its feet, the setting is particularly evocative. Little wonder that, when a young Walter Scott lived for a time with his grandparents at Sandyknowe Farm, the Tower and its surroundings cast a spell on him that was to shape his life.

And ever, by the winter hearth,
Old tales I heard of woe and mirth,
Of lovers' sleights, of ladies' charms,
Of witches' spells, and warriors' arms.

This was the setting for Scott's first published poem, 'The Eve of St John', a melodramatic tale in the style of a Border ballad, with murder, a suspicious husband who himself had a guilty secret and, of course, a ghost.

Scott came very close to never writing a word or collecting the ballads he published in *The Minstrelsy of the Scottish Borders*. The nursemaid who accompanied him to his grandparents' farm was so desperate to get back to her boyfriend in Edinburgh that she resolved to murder young Walter. But, as she later confessed, when the opportunity arose, she could not bring herself to do it. She was, of course, sent packing. After her departure, young Walter spent countless hours with Grandpa – 'Auld

Beardie' – and Sandy Bailie the cowherd. The legends and folktales they told him, supplemented by what he heard as a schoolboy in Kelso, inspired him to write poems and novels but also *Tales of Grandfather*, recounting in turn the stories of Scottish history for his own grandson.

Return to road junction, turn right and, at T junction, left (signed Kelso) and proceed to town centre.

Originally known as Calchau, Kelso takes its name from the chalky hill exposed by the Tweed as it rounds a sharp bend, now joined by the Teviot. Stone Age peoples gathered near the confluence of these two rivers on a regular basis and, judging by the size of a stone age timber building near Kelso, in fairly large numbers. When the Anglo Saxons arrived in the 7th century, there was already a settlement at Wester Kelso. This town co-existed for a time with Easter Kelso, which grew around the 12th century Abbey.

In medieval times, the two Kelsos were in the shadow of the Royal Burgh of Roxburgh, directly across the Tweed, and were very much its poor relations. That town had grown up around Marchidun Castle, later renamed Roxburgh Castle, built on a rocky knoll at the tip of land where the Tweed and the Teviot meet. Locally produced goods were sold in the Kelso market places, but Roxburgh had international trading privileges and even a licence to mint coins. The tug of war for Roxburgh Castle brought a great deal of trouble, especially when the Castle was occupied by the English. Both the Royal Burgh of Roxburgh and Wester Kelso went into a terminal decline after the Scots regained the castle in 1460 and demolished it rather than have it fall into English hands. Then, in 1492 Berwick-upon-Tweed ended up permanently on the English side of the border. Easter Kelso, later just Kelso, carried on as before servicing the needs of the Abbey, the wealthiest of the four Border abbeys until Henry VIII's troops reduced it to the remnants we see today. The monks put up a good fight but were killed in the attack, and the business they generated was gone overnight.

Despite the disruption associated with the Reformation and later attacks on the town, the people of Kelso stoically rebuilt the town from the rubble and recycled buildings that were still standing. They used one of the abbey buildings as their parish church until the roof fell in during a service, so fulfilling a prophecy made five centuries earlier by Thomas the Rhymer that the Abbey would fall 'when at its fullest'. It seems he was referring not to the institution, by then a distant memory, but the building.

Towards the end of the 16th century some of the most powerful families in the area realised that the reiving culture of tit-for-tat cattle stealing, and long running family feuds, was making things difficult and resolved to settle differences in a healthier way. And so, what became known as 'the Kelso Band' offered the hand of peace in 1596.

The Kelso Band

Burdened with responsibility for feeding their extended families and followers during the famines of the 1590s, the 'heid men' of the Home, Kerr, Douglas, Turnbull and other families, declared themselves fed up with the 'innumerable slaugchters, fyre raisings, heirschippis (reiving) and detesabill enormitie dailie committit'.

So they invited the heads of the main families they feuded with, amongst them the Armstrongs, Elliots, Bells and a branch of the Scotts, to give up these destructive habits. They, their wives, their children and their tenants had eight days to give their pledge. And, if they did not, it was business as usual.

Sadly, the families who received this invitation so distrusted the families who had extended it that they refused, and the reiving and blackmailing continued. The Kelso Band did however end one bloodily famous feud: Janet Scott married Thomas Kerr of Ferniehurst.

After the fall of Roxburgh Castle and as late as World War 1, Kelso was the regional muster point. In the words of Dorcas Symm, 'Now in the market square goes out the call/to fight with honour someone else's war'. Leslie mustered a Covenanting army there in 1639, then marched up the

Tweed to Philiphaugh to inflict a crushing defeat on a Royalist army. In 1715 Jacobites from all over Scotland and the north of England rallied here before setting off over the Cheviots to win back the crown for the Stuarts. They failed but, 30 years later, Bonnie Prince Charlie overnighted in Kelso on his way south to try again. That attempt very nearly succeeded.

By this time, Kelso was a significant producer of linen and was also processing locally grown tobacco. By the time abundant supplies from across the Atlantic made home production uneconomic, agricultural improvers had introduced other crops. The Georgian buildings surrounding the market square, the largest in Scotland, attest to the ability of Kelso's merchants to make money from the rising demand for goods, equipment and services.

For a while Kelso's schools also produced a bumper crop of eminent people. One of them, Thomas Pringle, a friend of Walter Scott's, campaigned for the abolition of slavery, becoming Secretary of the Anti-Slavery Society. Shrugging off the advice of friends, he courted controversy and law suits by employing a former slave, Mary Prince, and encouraged her to write her autobiography. Others whose interests lay in the latest scientific and technological advances used their knowledge to practical effect. Kelso man John Gibson earned himself the reputation of having uncanny, even wizardly powers.

A Shocking Way to Catch a Thief

A local laird once enlisted John Gibson's help to finding out who had stolen some sheep. He was pretty sure his shepherd was the culprit but had no proof. Could John Gibson try to get to the truth of the matter?

John agreed to give it a go and summoned the shepherd who, predictably, denied stealing the sheep. John then asked the man to take hold of a length of chain telling him that when the chain vibrated he would be able to name the thief.

The bemused man, thinking he had nothing to lose by going along with this daft notion, grasped the chain through which, by flicking a switch, Gibson delivered an electric shock. Believing this was magic or perhaps in a state of fright about what might happen next, the shepherd confessed.

Leaving the old town, we pass the scant remnants of Kelso Abbey and cross the Tweed by a sturdy bridge built to replace one washed away by floods. Memories of this bridge, designed by John Rennie who was to build London's Waterloo Bridge in similar style, helped lure Kelso poet, Will Ogilvie, back from Australia.

Sunlit or swept by winter's blast
The old bridge stands, a link between
The Abbey's hoar and wrinkled past
And the young elm-bud's waking green;

The nesting rooks above it wheel
From elm to elm on sable wings;
Beneath it, racing round the reel,
The line upon the bent rod sings.

Across the world hope's bridges bear
The wanderer's never-resting feet,
But peace and rest are mingled where
Earth's fairest rivers, mingling, meet.

Leave Kelso on B6352 (signed Yetholm) and proceed to Yetholm.

Heading out of town past Pinnacle Hill to our left, we pass the final resting place of people who lived on this south bank of the Tweed 4,000 years ago. But in 1542 the thoughts of James v's soldiers on this route to fight Henry viii's men at Haddon Rig (a battle they won), would have been for those who had fallen at nearby Flodden in 1513. Flodden is worth a detour if you have the heart and time, but if you lack one or other, the final verse of Will Ogilvie's poem, Flodden Hill, evokes the ghostly imprint of a long-ago battle on an innocent landscape:

Was there ever a trumpet calling?
Was there ever a troop road by?
Was it only the dead leaves falling
That wailed to a windy sky?
Is there no grass red and sodden?
No trampled field and trodden?
Is it only a dream of Flodden
Where silent the dead men lie?

We press on to Yetholm, or rather, Yetholms. Town Yetholm and Kirk Yetholm sit on opposite banks of the Bowmont. The tell-tale signs of Stone Age living 6,000 years ago such as, the Bronze Age shields recovered from Yetholm bog and the Iron Age cultivation terraces scarring the hills, tell us that this place attracted a succession of peoples. Yetholm owes its Cymric name to the Celtic British. The word 'yett', meaning a gate, is still used here.

It was to Town Yetholm in 1304 that Edward I of England, Hammer of the Scots, summoned Scottish nobles who had refused to recognise him as their own king's superior, to give them a second chance. For the next three centuries, Yetholm suffered badly at the hands of the English as they tried time and again to wrest control from the Scots.

Proceed to Kirk Yetholm.

Gypsies, or 'Egyptians' as they were then called, came to Kirk Yetholm in the 17th century and, unusually for a people who were by tradition nomadic, put down roots of sorts. There had been gypsies in Scotland since the late 15th or early 16th century. Travelling gypsy bands entertained with stories and songs as the medieval bards had done and gypsies were sometimes guests at the dinner tables of the rich and powerful. Johnnie Faa, was said for example, to be 'lovit' by King James IV.

Most gypsies sold small household items and herbal remedies, mended pots or told 'weirds' (fortunes) for small amounts of money, food or a place to spend the night. With a language and a culture of their own, they were viewed by many as a welcome addition to Scottish society, despite living by a code of honour often at odds with the law of the land.

Things changed abruptly in 1609 when King James VI of Scotland and I of England, no friend either to witches or reivers, passed an 'Act Anent Gypsies'. This banished gypsies from Britain unless they were prepared to give up their nomadic lifestyle. The majority stuck with their way of life and risked being caught – the men hung, women drowned and children branded.

Yetholm's Royal Gypsies

In the face of these oppressions, the descendants of Johnnie Faa left the Lothians and headed for the Cheviot Hills where they could, if necessary, melt away into the hills. By the early 18th century they had a permanent base in Yetholm to which they and other gypsy families returned after summer travelling to sit out the winter months in the relative comfort of Little Egypt.

There is more than one story about how they came by their cottages and land, but all are essentially the same – a gypsy kindness was rewarded by a grateful laird with tenants' rights which gave them, in the eyes of the law, the right to be treated as equals.

Until the late 19th century, the Yetholm gypsies had a hereditary King or Queen, and a Palace where coronations took place. Such was their fame that *The Scotsman* published a lament for Wull Faa, who died in 1847, which captured the spirit of this hospitable man. His distinguishing feature, a badly scarred hand, was the legacy of an adventure involving the theft from the English side of the Border of another kind of spirit – gin.

> *Though his hand held no sceptre, the stranger can tell,*
> *That the full bowl of welcome became it as well;*
> *The fisher the rambler, by burn or by brae,*
> *Ne'er from old Wullie's hallam went empty away*

On the old house at Yetholm we've sat at the board,
The guest, highly honoured, of Egypt's old lord;
And marked his eye glisten as oft as he told,
Of his feats on the border, his prowess of old.

Border gypsies though were prone to family feuds and settling scores with violence. Indeed, they lived by honour codes similar to those of the earlier reivers. Meg Merrilees in Walter Scott's novel *Guy Mannering* is modelled on Jean Gordon, the widow of Patrick Faa, whose nine sons, despite her best efforts, found themselves on the wrong side of the law and paid with their lives. She outlived all nine, the last three being hung for stealing sheep in 1730, 16 years before Jean herself was drowned by a mob in Carlisle for the offence of supporting Bonnie Prince Charlie.

The gypsies of Yetholm were not very different from many of those whose fortunes they read and to whom they sold their lucky charms. They had their children baptised and went to church but were simultaneously superstitious. And many people were loath to upset gypsies for fear of retribution. Even Will o' Phaup, James Hogg, the Ettrick Shepherd's grandfather, the last man in the Borders to speak with the fairies, was wary. Finding himself on the receiving end of their ire after he had inadvertently crossed them, he told his wife that he could have held his own with them if 'it hadna been for their warlockry'. And as one local laird discovered to his cost, it did not pay to rile a gypsy.

Gypsy Janet's Curse

In 1714 William Ker of Greenhead, in his role as judge, sentenced a Yetholm gypsy lad to a spell in Jedburgh Tolbooth. A few weeks later, the boy's family were themselves on trial for burning down William Ker's house at Springwood near Kelso in retribution. All were found guilty and sentenced. The lad's mother, Janet Stewart, was sentenced to be whipped four times in each of three public places in the town, imprisoned for three days, and then to be nailed by the left ear to a post near the market cross for 15 minutes.

Market places are busy, and in those 15 minutes Janet took the opportunity to lay a very public curse on William Ker. When Ker's only son died childless, it was whispered that this was the fulfilment of Janet's gypsy curse. Janet meanwhile, if she was still alive, was on the other side of the Atlantic. She and others of her family had been sentenced by William Ker to transportation as the final part of their punishment.

And what of Yetholm's residents who were not gypsies? Changes in farming left many who had previously had a bit of land without any. Some benevolent landowners like the Bennets, the Yetholm gypsies' landlord, rented cottages with a little land and grazing rights to people displaced in this way. They met their rent by working as day labourers or turning their hand to a trade or craft. While the population of some villages shrank, Yetholm's population grew and by 1776 there were 25 weavers in the village. They formed their own guild and took for their motto a sobering line from the Bible: 'Men's days are swifter than a weaver's shuttle'.

Yetholm was however bypassed by the industrial revolution. The Bowmont River had a habit of washing away the latest rickety wooden bridge and cutting communications between Town Yetholm and Kirk Yetholm but it was not large or fast flowing enough to drive mechanised spinning and weaving equipment.

When John Baird was taken on as the new minister in the late 1820s this was a neglected corner of the Borders. He had grown up nearby but had travelled a bit since then and, now in his early 30s, brought a reforming zeal that was infectious. Within ten years of his appointment, funds had been found to build a stone bridge over the Bowmont, a new kirk and a school, and to pay a teacher. He was the prime mover in efforts to work with the gypsy community, initially in Yetholm and later across Scotland, to give gypsy children the opportunity of schooling. By 1843, more than a quarter of Yetholm school's 90 pupils were gypsies.

Return to Town Yetholm and, at junction with B6401, turn left (signed Jedburgh) then, at junction with B6436, turn right (signed Kelso), continue up hill and turn left at sign for Linton Church.

Stone plaque above entrance to Linton Church

Once a much bigger village, Linton goes back to the Stone Age or earlier. The Tryst, the site of standing stones and once a gathering place of Neolithic peoples, later became a rallying point for Border reivers starting out on cross border raids. The site of Linton Church on its grassy knoll is itself the subject of local lore. The knoll was created by two sisters who were set the task of sifting enough sand on which to build a church as a penance. Some say that they were doing penance not for themselves but for their brother who had killed a priest, and that their labour spared him from execution. Others believe that the sisters were themselves responsible for the deaths of 50 men whose skulls were found in a single grave in the grounds of the churchyard. If that was so, it was some fight because most had died violently.

Linton is also associated with another legend, the subject of the stone carving above the door of the church. This one involves the slaying of a dragon-like monster.

The Worm of Linton

A long time ago a giant worm made its lair on the side of Linton Hill and lived for centuries on a self-service diet of local cattle. No one knew where this monstrous creature had come from, but it was greatly feared. It was three Scots yards long and thicker than a man's leg, and so getting rid of it was not going to be easy. Robert Davidson, a ploughman poet from neighbouring Morebattle takes up the tale:

> When roused by hunger, destructive it roam'd,
> And each thing it met with, it quickly intomb'd:
> Rewards had been offer'd the monster to kill,
> Yet still it had baffled all courage and skill

Nothing thrown at it from a distance could pierce its scaly skin but eventually, one young man screwed up enough courage to grab a broadsword and a lance, mount a horse and approach the monster. Some, Davidson included, say this brave young buck was Eliot of Lariston while others, including most historians, say it was John Somerville, whose family owned lands around Linton. Whoever it was, he enraged the monster further by jabbing at it with his sword and lance to no avail. But then he:

> ...turn'd from the monster, unawed by its might,
> But quickly returned in invincible plight:
> Of hot burning turf he prepared a red roll,
> Bound fast with green willows, and stuck on a pole;
> When, with its vast jaws, to inclasp him it strove,
> Down the throat of the monster the faggot he drove.

The worm roared in pain and retreated, mortally wounded, into its lair. With the worm gone for good, the bold Somerville, or perhaps Eliot, was lauded as a hero. It was Somerville, however, who was rewarded with the Barony of Linton.

Burning peat on the tip of a lance was not an uncommon sight in the Borders at one time. March Law specified a process for retrieving stolen goods known as Hot Trod. This allowed the victims five days to carry out a counter-raid to get their, gear, back provided the rider at the head of the party carried a lance with a burning peat on the tip signalling that a hot trod was in progress.

Return to B6401 T junction and turn right (signed Morebattle).

The journey from Linton to Morebattle is a short one today but, until the local rivers altered their course, the two villages were separated by a shallow lake. Thanks to new drainage technology, the boggy but fertile ground left behind became prime arable land in the 19th century. The farmers here were among the earliest and most enthusiastic innovators of the agricultural revolution. Dawson of Frogden for example not only experimented with drainage and use of marl to fertilise soil, but also worked out how to grow turnips in quantities that enabled him to keep cattle and sheep alive over the winter. By the end of the century the Merse was producing enough grain to satisfy local demand and send the surplus to London.

By this time, farm labour was hired on six-month contracts and supplemented seasonally by men and women hired by the day or week. It was a way of life that ploughman-poet Robert Davidson, a contemporary of James Hogg, knew well. His poems illuminate not only how those employed on the land lived, but also how they were affected by and felt about the changes they lived through. His poem 'Term Day' captures the scene and mood on the day a hind and his bondager wife, packed up to go to their next contract or 'fee'.

> *The thriftie housewife packs her brittle ware,*
> *The stools and forms are a' turn'd oot o'doors.*
> *They in an instant make the cottage bare*

The accommodation provided for farm labourers in Davidson's time was poor. Amongst the prized possessions labourers took from place to place there might be a door or a pane of glass. Davidson's awareness of how their standard of living compared with that of their employers came from personal experience. He gives voice to his views on that subject in these lines from the poem:

Ye sons o' affluence, sae fully fed,
Let pity's eye look softly on their pain,
Who're doom'd to labour for their scanty bread,
An' a wee bit shed to hide their head.

And even more politically:

How sad these lands where mankind cannot make
A change of masters, and a change of toil!
But, by a despot's chain, as to a stake,
The hapless peasant's tethered to the soil.

Another of his poems, Kirn Day, describes the scene on the last day of harvesting. Having cut the farmer's corn, the labourers get to glean the last ears from the last stalks of corn to keep for themselves. While they glean, an 'aged matron' entertains with stories of deeds –

Perform'd by warlocks in the lonely glen;
Converting broomsticks into stately steeds,
To scour the wilds, unscared by march or fen;
Or what mishaps befell on festive nights,
In days of yore of which our minstrels sing;
How unperceiv'd approach'd the fairy knights,
And stole the boasted beauties from the ring,
Then fled to fairy-land on viewless wing.

And once the work was done, a feast and high jinks among the young while their elders recall the olden days of warriors and reivers, and the revellers agree how much better things are now in lawful times. But, Davidson concludes:

> *See ruined hamlets in his track appear!*
> *In distant lands their former inmates mourn.*

Agricultural progress did result in people having to leave the area. Those who stayed had no option but to adapt to new ways. They did not however accept other changes imposed on them without protest. Covenanters here were many and several local men were executed for their part in an uprising in 1679. Later, Morebattle was the scene of riot in 1725. It was sparked by a change in the way church ministers were appointed but was at heart about changes in the relationship between lairds and people after the 1707 Union of the Parliaments. Their social contract of protection in return for working service was crumbling.

The Morebattle Riot

The Patronage Act of 1712 gave parish heritors, usually the local lairds, power to appoint new Church of Scotland ministers without consulting parishioners. This was seen as an attack on Presbyterian democracy and also as a move towards making the church subject to the state – the very things the Covenanters of the previous century had resisted.

In 1725, the Duke of Roxburgh chose a new minister, a Mr Christie, for the people of Morebattle without consultation. Robert Davidson describes in 'The Ordination' how the folk of Morebattle gathered in the kirkyard to prevent their new minister being appointed and introduced to the congregation:

> *That day in every face was seen,*
> *Of those assembled on the green,*
> *A discontented air.*
> *Of pastor they no more had choice,*
> *Since law had hush'd the public voice,*
> *And said they must submit;*

Twas vain objections, then, to make,
Since they must for their pastor take,
Whome'er his Grace thought fit.

The mob was urged on by a man called Nub of Beaumont, whose rabble-rousing address was followed by a rush to break into the church. When the ordination party arrived and were unable to enter the church, they tried reasoning with the angry parishioners. Tempers flared, fighting broke out and the laird and the ordination party retreated.

But that was not the end of the story. Indeed, it was a pyrrhic victory for those who barred the way. Determined not to be thwarted, the ordination party made their way to Linton Church and conducted the service there. As for the rioters:

They now perceived the thought was vain
Rights to acquire, or to retain,
By reckless deeds of strife;
For right or wrong, the law prevailed,
The presentée was there installed,
Their minister for life.

Some of the ringleaders were subsequently arrested and gaoled for causing disorder. Rather more happily, Mr Christie turned out to be a good minister and was taken to the hearts of his parishioners.

Over in Maxton, a similar face-off between the parishioners and an ordination party took place but was diffused when Ramsey, Kelso's minister, addressed the mob saying 'You beat us last time; and, my wig being lost, I had to ride home with a bare pow! But to-day I am better provided – I have got a spare one in my pocket!'. And, out of his pocket he pulled the said wig and waved it at the crowd. They roared with laughter and parted to allow the ordination party into the church.

The issue of how the church was run simmered on in Morebattle. Only 14 years later, in 1739, John Hunter, who may have been present at Christie's ordination, became the first Secession minister in Scotland. Having left the Church of Scotland, he had no church and, as in the days of the Covenanters, held meetings outside until a new church was built in Town Yetholm.

Support for the seceding churches remained strong. Three thousand gathered at nearby Gateshaw to celebrate the centenary of Hunter's appointment. Their choice of Gateshaw was significant – it was an old Covenanter meeting place where, every 50 years, an outdoor or 'blanket preaching' still takes place. The large numbers attending in 1839 was a sign of things to come. Four years later, tensions within the Church of Scotland reached such a pitch that around a third of the remaining ministers voted with their feet in what came to be known as 'the Disruption', which established the Free Church of Scotland.

Leaving Morebattle take first public road on left (signed Cessford).

Approaching the sturdy remains of Cessford Castle, built with four-metre thick walls for a branch of the Ker family, it is hard to believe that it was captured by the English in 1523. In 1607, four years after the Union of the Crowns, the Kers abandoned it as it was no longer fit for purpose.

Long before then the Kerrs, originally a Norman family, became one of the most powerful clans in this part of the Borders. The family tree put down firm roots and had, by the 15th century, sprouted several sturdy branches. The Kers of Cessford lived within six miles of the 'kery-powed' (left-handed) Kerrs of Ferniehurst. The two branches of the family fought constantly, stopping only to fight alongside one another against the English. So great was the animosity between them that the Cessford branch dropped an 'r' from their name to distance themselves from the two 'r' Kerrs at Ferniehurst.

Some of their spats with other prominent Border families went on for decades as well. Walter Kerr of Cessford was banished to France for his part in the murder of Walter Scott in 1552, an act carried out to avenge Walter Scott's killing of Ker's father at the Battle of Melrose Bridge – a quarter of a century earlier. Despite their feuds and vendettas, the Kers of Cessford were considered trustworthy enough to be appointed as wardens of the Middle March for the Scottish side of the border. And it was in that role that William Ker in 1581 extended hospitality to an interesting visitor.

Border Hospitality

One evening a man came to William's door, seeking a night's hospitality, and saying only that he was travelling from England to Edinburgh to deliver a message. William knew that James VI and his court were in Edinburgh, so he asked no more and welcomed the weary traveller indoors. The wardens of the Marches were frequently asked to extend the hospitality of their house to travellers on diplomatic missions.

At dinner, it was usual for diners to remove their hats before they came to the table. This visitor did not, however, remove his. What might sound to us like simple bad manners, could easily have cost the man his life. It was disrespectful but, by keeping his hat on, he was telling his hosts that he was a Roman Catholic. This was a decidedly risky thing to do, because allegiance to the Roman Catholic Church had by this time been outlawed.

William, a Presbyterian Scot, was well aware of this, but chose to ignore the hat and signalled for the meal to be served. The traveller enjoyed his hospitality and went on his way the next day having been tacitly granted safe passage on the next leg of his journey.

It later came to light that their guest's mission in coming to Scotland was to plead with the young King James VI to grant asylum to Roman Catholics who were being hounded out of England. We can only speculate about why William chose to turn a blind eye to the offending hat.

Despite their many misdemeanours, the Kers of Cessford enjoyed royal favour. They were granted vast tracts of land in the middle ages, elevated to Earls in the early 17th century, and in 1704 were given the title of Duke of Roxburgh, playing an important role in the Union of England and Scotland.

Loop around castle and farm to return to B6401 and turn left (signed Kelso).

We join the road just below where the Kale Water joins the Teviot. As at other confluences, ancient peoples met and gathered here. Three bronze shields retrieved from Eckford Moss were probably offerings made to gods worshipped by the local Celtic British tribes.

Turn right at the T junction onto A698 (signed Kelso).

We re-enter Kelso at Maxwellheugh where the railway station was once situated. This was inconvenient for townspeople particularly during the first four years of the railway's operation. They not only had to cross Rennie's Bridge to get to the station but also pay a bridge toll for the privilege. Locals began to suspect that the cost of building the bridge, after an earlier one was washed away, had been covered and that greed had got the better of those charged with paying down the debt. Suspicions grew and allegations flew until, in 1854, there was a riot. The tolls were abolished and prosecutions and convictions followed.

Following signs for St Boswells and Springwood turn left before Tweed bridge onto A699 (signed St Boswells).

Swinging around the Border Union Agricultural Society showground, with the Tweed on the right, we skirt the world-renowned salmon fishing Junction Pool where the Teviot joins the Tweed. Crossing the bridge across the Teviot onto the narrow strip of land between that river and the Tweed, we pass Kelso's Trysting Tree on the right. Every year, during the riding of the Kelso marches, the Callant dismounts here to cut his initials in the sod, recalling the days when the reivers did this to let followers know that they had gone ahead and in what direction. Trysting trees were often chosen for their association with magic and fairies, and were rallying points for others too. Lawyers and clients met to seal deals and lovers to carve initials in the bark of the tree.

On the far bank of the Tweed sits Floors Castle on land that once belonged to Kelso Abbey, and where Wester Kelso stood. The Castle was built for and remains in the hands of descendants of the Kers of Cessford. The Kers, like many of their fellow landowners, gave up their draughty stone towers in the more settled 18th century and moved into luxurious accommodation built, decorated and furnished in the fashion of the day. The Duke had done very well out of the Union negotiations and wanted the best money could buy, so William Adam, the star Scottish architect of the day, was hired to design his palace. It was later expanded to a design by William Playfair.

Back on this side of the Tweed, the road curves around a grassy mound, site of the once mighty Roxburgh Castle with the royal burgh at its feet. For more than four centuries this place was filled from dawn to dusk with the sights, sounds and smells of busy activity. It was also the most contested piece of land in Scotland. The politicking and dirty tricks that went on to gain or regain this castle are too many to relate but two tales stand out. The first is the story of how the Black Douglas, as he was known in England, or Good Sir James as he was known in Scotland, recaptured the castle in 1313 after the English had held it for eight years. This was one of Walter Scott's favourite episodes in his *Tales of a Grandfather*.

The Climbing Cows

Roxburgh Castle was in a good defensive position but was not invincible. And in 1313 James Douglas had a motive to prove that! Edward I of England had taken captive Mary, Robert the Bruce's sister, and had the poor woman living for a time in a cage hung over the battlements of the castle exposed to the elements and public view.

James Douglas was a smart man. For one thing, he chose a feast day to attack. It was Fastern Eve or Shrove Tuesday, the festival celebrated before Lent. It was traditional to eat and drink well on this day in anticipation of six weeks of frugal eating, so he reckoned the castle would be lightly guarded and the watchmen none too vigilant. As the sun set and the light began to fade, James gave the signal to his waiting men. They wrapped themselves in their black cloaks and, bent over to look like black cattle, crept towards the castle.

Meanwhile, a soldier's wife was walking her wakeful baby on the battlements. Seeing the cattle far below, she remarked to the watchman, 'Is it no late for cattle to be oot without a herd tae mind them?' 'Aye lass', replied the watchman, 'But they'll no be there long if the Black Douglas is aboot.' Little did he know!

The woman went back to walking her baby and the watchman dozed off. Meanwhile, the 'cattle' crept closer. Then they started to climb the walls. They could hear the woman singing to her baby as they clambered over the parapet. 'Hush ye, Hush ye, little pet ye, the Black Douglas will no get ye', she sang until, right behind her, she heard a deep voice say, 'I wouldnae be sae sure o' that'.

She no doubt thought the watchman was teasing her, but turning around she came face to face with the Black Douglas himself. The Scots took the Castle that night, but it was said that the Black Douglas took the woman and her baby under his protection. What happened to the baby's father hardly bears thinking about, but we know from other stories that James Douglas, although he did some terrible things, did have a soft side.

The second tale also involves a Scottish attempt to regain Roxburgh Castle, this time by the more conventional method of laying siege and bombarding it with cannon. This attempt too was successful but had a less than happy outcome both for James II, who was leading the Scottish troops, and the castle.

Dead Man Captures a Castle

The year was 1460. James II had drawn up his troops and set up his cannon in the grounds of what is now Floors Castle. The siege was going well when one of the cannons, instead of firing its charge at the castle, exploded, thus scattering jagged pieces of metal in all directions. One of these lodged in the king's leg and in no time, he was dead. Shocked and leaderless, his nobles halted the siege. That you might think would be the end of this attempt to recapture the castle.

However, James's Queen, Mary of Gueldres, and their eight-year-old son, had received word that the siege was going well and were on their way to join the king when a messenger delivered the news that her husband had been badly wounded. Mary and young James hurried on but by the time they arrived on the battle field, James II was dead.

Realising that the siege had been all but won when the cannon had exploded, Mary stepped out in front of the stunned nobles and their troops, urging them to fight on with, in Scott's telling, the words, 'Let it not be said that such brave champions needed to hear from a woman, a widowed one at that, the courageous advice and comfort she ought rather to have had from you'.

Then off she went, her young son at her heels, to arrange a hasty coronation. Whatever she said to James's nobles, they were galvanised or shamed into action and resumed the siege. A few days later they had taken Roxburgh Castle for their new king, James III.

And so it was that Thomas the Rhymer's prophecy that a dead man would win Roxburgh Castle was fulfilled. Mary, however, ordered that the castle be demolished to prevent it falling into English hands again. When the English next captured the castle, they took possession of a pile of rubble. Back in Edinburgh Mary raised Trinity College Kirk as a beautiful memorial in stone to her lost James.

Local poet John Leyden later described the ghostly scene at Roxburgh.

Fallen are thy towers; and where the palace stood,
In gloomy grandeur waves yon hanging wood.
Crushed are thy halls, save where the peasant sees
One moss-clad ruin rise between the trees.

And what of the Royal Burgh? It had been at the heart of David I's plans to build a prosperous Scotland, but, when the Castle fell, the town lost customers and protection. The taking of Berwick upon Tweed by the English in 1482 was the final straw. Stripped of its status as a Royal Burgh and irretrievably damaged by warfare, the remaining residents upped sticks. The once vibrant burgh became a ghost town. Its wooden buildings rotted away and sank beneath the turf. Only the name survived – it travelled down the Teviot to begin again in a new location.

Our road runs on through rich land once worked by many hands offering, from this south side of the Tweed, wonderful views of Smailholm Tower and the Eildons to the north. First, however, we pass Makerstoun Trows, a 150-metre bar of volcanic rock broken by a few slits through which the waters of the Tweed force their way downstream. A local legend explains how the bar and the slits in it came to be there.

The Making of Makerstoun Trows

Michael Scot the Wizard once had occasion to chase a fleeing imp who had done something to anger him down the Tweed. The chase began upriver. Knowing that wizards are powerless on or in water, the quick-thinking imp hastily fashioned a boat out of the head of a shovel to make a quick getaway and set off down the river. Michael meanwhile gave chase in a boat that he had 'borrowed' from the Monks of Melrose, who would be none too pleased. They were already suspicious of his mutterings in unfamiliar languages thinking he was making spells or invoking spirits.

Now Michael knew that he was unable to use his powers on water, but figured if he could overtake the imp he might just be able to stop him getting away. Somewhere around Mertoun, his boat overtook the imp's improvised shovel boat, and Michael sped on downstream. Some say he had help from the witch on nearby Corbie's Crag who transformed herself into a crow and swooped down to slow the imp's progress, but at any rate the wizard reached Makerstoun first.

Out he jumped onto the bank and began the spell that would create a bar of rock to stop the imp going any further. Speed was of the essence. Indeed, he was in such a rush that, as he worked his way out from the bank, building the bar bit by bit, his foot caught the water of the Tweed and interfered with his magic. As the imp got closer he couldn't believe his luck – there were slits in the rock to allow the water through. He paddled for all he was worth, steered his shovel boat through one of them, and was off down river leaving Michael standing.

And so, the Makerstoun Trows remind us of the day an imp got the better of Michael Scot.

Rutherford, the family from which the next place takes its name, claims to be the second oldest in the Borders – only the Swintons are older. Legend says they were named for the nearby ford over the Tweed after an Anglo-Saxon ancestor crossed the river with his king on his back to do battle with a Celtic war band. The Rutherfords later moved closer to Jedburgh but lived for a time at nearby Littledean Tower. The ruins are worth a visit on foot (*after Broomhouse right turn for Ploughlands and park*) not least for the tower's unusual design and dramatic setting, but also its association with a number of ghost stories.

The Laird of Littledean

Throughout the 18th Century the ghostly forms of two well-dressed ladies were often seen in a particular three cornered field at Bowbrigsyke walking arm in arm. No one knew why they favoured that spot until roadmen repairing the nearby road found the skeletons of two young women. They had been laid under flat stones used, until a bridge was built, to cross the burn.

The grim discovery confirmed the long-held suspicion that the ghostly women were the sisters of Harry Gilles, one time Laird of Littledean. Speculation about why the two women had disappeared at the same time was rife. Perhaps they had sickened and died at Littledean? Or perhaps they had been the victims of their brother's violent temper? It was rumoured that shortly before they disappeared, they had been seen trying to protect a young girl their brother had taken a fancy to when they were out walking. Finding their skeletons all these years later confirmed their sad fate, though not sadly, the identity of their killer or indeed, if she existed, the girl. That these two ghosts were never seen again suggests that being found was enough to give them peace.

By a curious twist of fate this bully of a man later fell to his own death from a nearby point on the steep river banking. Before his death, however, Harry Gillis had another vengeful encounter that had tongues wagging. This time the woman was a witch – or so Harry Gillis said.

His story was that he was out with his hunting dogs when they went after a hare but suddenly stopped in their tracks for no reason he could see, and the hare got away. When the dogs refused to go on he muttered to himself that the hare must be one of the witches rumoured to live nearby. No sooner were the words out of his mouth, when hares sprang from nowhere and everywhere and surrounded his horse. His dogs stood still as if entranced. In a terrible rage, Gillis killed his dogs one by one. The last dog however ran at the biggest hare and drove it back towards him. Just when it looked like the chase was over, the hare leapt up over his horse's neck. Gillis drew his knife and cut off its foreleg as it passed. The injured hare limped off into the trees followed by all the others. The Laird picked up the hare's foreleg and went home with his sole remaining dog.

However, when he heard that a woman in Maxton had lost her forearm in an accident, he grabbed the severed foreleg and went to her house, convinced that there was witchcraft at work. By the time he got there, the foreleg had become a woman's lower arm – and it was a perfect fit for the bleeding stump on the woman's arm. Urged on by Harry Gilles, the young men of Maxton dragged the woman out of her house that very day and drowned her as a witch.

It was said that for the rest of his miserable life, Harry Gilles was tormented by a phantom hand that bore more than a passing resemblance to the one he had taken to the house of the woman he had accused. Perhaps she was a witch! Sadly, having suffered the fate of so many accused of witchcraft, the woman was never given the chance to tell her side of the story.

Leaving tragic Littledean and its dastardly laird behind, we come next to Maxton, once a town with a population significantly bigger than neighbouring St Boswells. The St Cuthbert's Way walking route passes through the village, and we drive over an old well dedicated to Cuthbert.

Just beyond Maxton is a signpost to Temple where long ago there was a 'hospitium', a hospital and travellers rest run by Knights Templar. This religious order came into existence to provide protection for men who went to the Crusades in the dual capacity of pilgrims visiting the Holy Land and soldiers fighting to gain control of Jerusalem from 'the Saracens', or Muslims. The belief that crusading armies could win control of 'the Holy Land' waned from the mid-13th century making the Knights Templar redundant. Over time they had amassed great wealth and consequently wielded considerable power behind the scenes but were now outlawed and forced to abandon this and other sites.

Back in the 21st century, we next pass a sign to Benrig Cemetery where the Harewell is located. This has nothing to do with Harry Gilles of Littledean's encounter with hares. 'Hare' here means holy. St Boisil himself may have drawn water from this well to heal those who sought his help. And as the spring feeding it is rich in minerals, especially iron, it may have helped restore ailing people to health. The story of St Boisil and St Boswells belongs to another journey. For now, we leave the last word with Thomas Pringle of Kelso, one of many who emigrated from this area:

Farewell to bonnie Teviotdale,
And Cheviot mountains blue,
The sail is flapping o'er the foam,
That bears me far from you.

At T junction with A68 turn right (signed Edinburgh) and follow road signs to Tweedbank Station.

Journey 6
Teviotdale

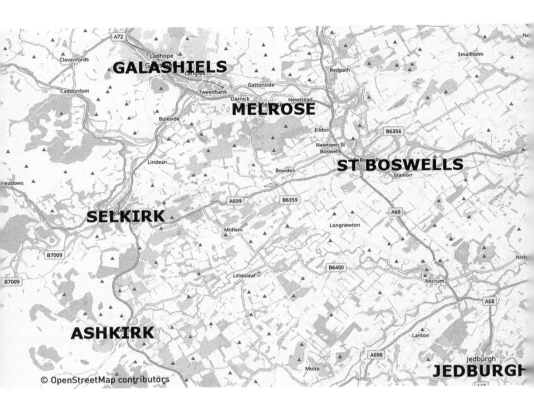

Our final journey is one of two distinct halves and contrasting landscapes. We go south to the Cheviot Hills through a red and gold sandstone landscape peppered with extinct volcanoes, returning north through uplands of older greywacke rock bordering Nithsdale and the Ettrick valley.

The early history of Teviotdale is similar to neighbouring dales. The area was already well populated when the Romans drove Dere Street through the lands of the Gadeni, whose domain straddled the Cheviot Hills, then north through the middle of Teviotdale, with the Selgovae to the west and the Votadini to the east. The Anglo-Saxon Northumbrians took little interest in western upland Teviotdale, but in the low-lying lands to the east Anglo Saxon villages sprang up.

The foundation of burghs and abbeys with the related social and economic changes brought in by Norman nobles gave new vitality to this part of the Tweed valley. Proximity to the border made it vulnerable to attack and occupation, and for the next four centuries the people of Teviotdale suffered the consequences of national conflicts slugged out on their doorsteps. Unsurprisingly, Teviotdale had numerous peel towers and some formidable castles. They and their owners though proved powerless against Henry VIII's mid-16th century ravaging of Border towns and villages. The Scottish Reformation added to the turbulence. These were tense and lawless times during which Teviotdale, controlled by an oligarchy of Kerrs, Scotts and Douglases, became the epicentre of the reiving world.

By the time James VI of Scotland was crowned King of England in 1603, Teviotdale, Ettrick and Yarrow were virtually ungovernable. James seriously considered creating a Middleshire out of the lands straddling the Cheviots and dispensing with the border, but chose instead to pass the 1609 act 'to purge the mydele schyres of this isle, heirtofoir callit the bordouris of Scotland and England, of that barbarous crueltie, wickednes and incivilitie whilk be inveterat custome almaist wes become naturall to mony of the inhabitantis thairof'.

Reiving did die out in the 17th century but new tensions built up as religious and political issues split communities, and volatile conditions led to witch-hunts. People had believed in witches and wizards for centuries, if not millennia, but the Witchcraft Act of 1563 made being a witch, or consulting with witches, a capital crime. Criminalising witchcraft was one means by which the Protestant Church tried to eradicate beliefs and practises which had previously rubbed along with those of the Roman Catholic Church. Famines and plagues made neighbour suspicious of neighbour, and everyone suspicious of people who supplied folk remedies or behaved in any way strangely. These were unpredictable times – ideal conditions for blaming a witch when things went wrong. At the height of the witch hunts between the 1590s and the 1660s, more witches were taken to trial and killed, relative to population size, in Scotland than any other part of Europe.

Much of the physical evidence of settlement in parts of Teviotdale has been obliterated by changes in land management which began mid-18th century. Redistribution of population followed with the mechanisation of textile production. Whole villages disappeared while others, notably Hawick, mushroomed into towns. No part of Scotland owes a bigger debt of gratitude to sheep than Teviotdale! Indeed, Allan Ramsay's quaintly named *Tea Table Miscellany*, a 18th century collection of songs in Scots, included 'Tarry Woo', describing the journey of wool from one wearer to another:

> *Tarry woo, tarry woo*
> *Tarry woo is ill tae spin;*
> *Card it weil, card it weil,*
> *Card it weil, ere ye begin.*
> *When it's cardit, row'd and spun,*
> *Then the work is halflins done;*
> *But when woven, dressed and clean,*
> *It may be cleadin' for a queen.*

Many Teviotdale men and women had to leave. Those who went overseas retained an affection for the area, often expressed in verse. Indeed, the area produced so many talented wordsmiths, thinkers and scientists in the 18th and early 19th centuries as to create a 'Teviotdale Enlightenment'. Besides poetry, Teviotdale has a wealth of folktales and Border ballads telling of the triumphs of Teviotdale's warriors and reivers. Several of these have an emphasis on looking out for friends and honouring obligations. But there are fewer songs of love lost and won than in Ettrick or Yarrow.

On this journey, we meet a ghostly wedding guest, bold reivers, fairies, reformers, witches and a 'keryhanded' family. And we hear how a mythical heroine fought to the death, how riverside rocks reveal the story of the earth, and how a herd of cows tripled in a matter of days.

The Journey: 86 miles

From Tweedbank Station follow signs to A68 south (signed Jedburgh).

Heading south, travellers get their first sight of all three Eildon Hills, a magnificent backdrop for Newtown St Boswells. Newtown (the St Boswells tag came later) is much older than its name suggests, owing its existence to water and to Dryburgh Abbey, on the other side of the Tweed. The Bowden Burn was the nearest suitable for milling grain while Monksford provided a way to get the grain and other supplies across the river.

Many villages in the area shrank as 19th century agricultural changes reduced the numbers needed to farm. Textile mills and the colonies lured others away. Newtown, however, bucked the trend. With the coming of the railways, it became a regional railhead for cattle and sheep. And after the last train rolled down the tracks in the late 1960s along with the bustle, noise and smells of its four-legged freight, the town reinvented itself again when it became the headquarters of Borders Regional Council.

Barely a step down the road is St Boswells, an old friend from Journeys 1 and 5. Our road skirts the town but cuts through a wide sward of common land that has belonged to the village since the first phase of its life as 'Lessudden'. The original village migrated from its flood prone position to the current site, but the survival of the common land with its cricket pitch and tennis courts, testifies to the determination of the folk of St Boswells to keep and use it for the commonweal.

South of St Boswells, the A68 runs for a while directly on top of a rollercoaster section of Dere Street which brings to mind Matt McGinn's song 'The Rolling Hills of the Border'.

When I die bury me low
Where I can hear the bonnie Tweed flow;
Sweeter place I never did know
The rolling hills o' the border

Nearby Longnewton was the birthplace in 1785 of writer and poet John Younger. Once a large village, it all but disappeared in his lifetime, its residents forced to find new work and homes – in his case as a shoemaker in St Boswells. While many of his contemporaries travelled the world for inspiration, John Younger, like James Hogg, had a living to make and stayed put in the Borders. He added the subtitle 'Robinson Crusoe Untravelled' to his memoirs, revealing that he was in a sense marooned between the world he came from and the literary one to which he aspired. While Walter Scott was embraced by the literary world, Younger, whose origins were much humbler and his politics diametrically opposed to those of Scott, was neither embraced nor celebrated. Scott was gentry and establishment. Younger however took issue with the Laird of Abbotsford's stance on land rights, church-state relations and foreign policy (they lived through the French Revolution and the Napoleonic Wars). Nor did he like Scott's portrayal of the Borders:

Our Walter Scott-ish fifty volumed taste,
Of ages dark, as windowless and dull –
His gothic holes, his barons, abbeys, priests,
Bows, beads, portcullisses, moats water-full.

Cresting a hill at Lilliard's Edge, Teviotdale lies before us. Here the Battle of Ancrum Moor was fought in 1545 and, against the odds, won by Border Scots whose knowledge of the terrain helped them to get the better of a 5,000 strong English army.

Lilliard's Edge acquired its name from a story that went around after the battle. When Lilliard, a local lass, heard that her young lover had fallen during the battle, she waded into the fray to avenge his death. She fought so fearlessly that, in the words on the monument at Lilliards Edge, 'even when her legs were cuttit off she fought upon her stumps.' Who Lilliard was, if indeed she existed, is a mystery. The name and history of this place is older than the woman for whom it is said to be named. Lilyot's Cross, on the exposed watershed of the Tweed and Teviot, was one of the designated places where Wardens of the Scottish and English Middle March met on truce days to settle cross border disputes.

Turn left onto minor road (signed Fairnington).

This road takes us to a small loch, home at times to a colony of swans, overlooked by Down Law. The building perched on the top of the Law is an observatory erected in the 18th century by Baron Rutherford of Fairnington. Later dubbed The Baron's Folly, there was little folly about Rutherford. The Scottish Enlightenment had people talking, thinking and writing about how society and the economy functioned, and about science and the application of new knowledge. The mindset and interests of Border lairds were changing. Rutherford's for example led him to pioneer fresh ways of potato growing and storage.

Turn first right after the loch.

Looming up before us is the Waterloo Monument at Peneil Heugh. It commemorates Britain's victory over the French at that battle. Wellington's victory brought the Napoleonic Wars to an end without the French ever making it onto British soil. The threat of French invasion had however been very real.

The False Alarm

The age-old early warning system of bale fires on the top of prominent hills with sight lines one to the other was the signal for fighting men to head for their local muster point. One such fire was lit on Peniel Heugh in 1804.

Further up the Teviot, Lord Minto, the man appointed to command the muster at Jedburgh, received a message that the bale fire on the Heugh had been lit. If the French had been spotted off the east coast, there was no time to be lost. As soon as his horse was saddled, Minto set off for Jedburgh by the most direct route possible – across the Teviot which was on that day in spate. He decided to risk the crossing.

But by the time Minto reached Jedburgh, so too had the news that it was a false alarm. The watchmen at Hume Castle had mistaken the fires of charcoal burners on the Northumberland coast for a bale fire, then lit their fire and triggered the Peniel Heugh fire. A soggy Lord Minto must have had a few choice words to say about the watchmen of Hume and what became known as the False Alarm!

A walk up to the monument (allow an hour and a half) yields panoramic views up and down the Teviot, south to the Cheviots and north across Lilyot's Cross to the Eildons and the Lammermuirs. As 'JBN', author of 'On Peniel Heugh', wrote:

Whoever climbs thee on a summer's day
And on the weather-beaten summit stands
A glorious outlook over fertile lands
And heath clad hills his labour shall repay
For full five counties 'neath him are unrolled
With silver streams and forests tipped with gold.

Proceed to T junction and turn right.

This road goes past stately Monteviot House in whose gardens there was once a spittal – hospital and hostel for devout travellers. Although the Kerrs of Ferniehurst were frequently at loggerheads with their relatives, the Kers of nearby Cessford, both families wielded enormous influence in Teviotdale before and after the Union of the Parliaments in 1707. Both had a knack of being on the winning side in conflicts, hanging onto or acquiring land, and successfully positioning family members in royal households. This gained them prestigious and powerful appointments locally and nationally. On occasion, it also ensured that hot-headed family members got away with murder. The rift between the two families was eventually bridged by the daughter of one marrying a son of the other to become Lord and Lady Lothian.

Passing Harestanes, now a visitor centre but named for a long gone stone circle, we rejoin the A68.

At T junction turn right (signed Edinburgh) then immediately left onto B6400 (signed Ancrum).

Ancrum sits in the crook of the Ale Water as it swings round to join the Teviot. Three-thousand-year old cup and ring marks in the area suggest people gathered here long before the Celtic British gave it its Cymric name. The village, laid out around a triangular green with its ancient mercat cross is however typically Anglo Saxon. Teviotdale's ecclesiastical affairs were overseen by the Archbishop of Glasgow between the 12th and 16th centuries and Ancrum, on the easterly edge of their domain, was the site chosen for a Bishops Palace. Long gone, the palace would have hosted important and, as the Roman Catholic Church crumbled during the Reformation, difficult meetings.

During the turbulent years leading up to and following the Reformation, the caves along the banks of the Ale became hiding places for soldiers, outlaws and, in the 17th century, Covenanters fleeing the militia sent to break up their outdoor gatherings. Support for the Covenanters was particularly strong around Ancrum. The writings of Samuel Rutherford from nearby Nisbet influenced the political history of the United Kingdom, proving that the pen in the long run is mightier than the sword.

Samuel Rutherford's Pen

Samuel Rutherford was only three years old in 1603 when James VI of Scotland became James I of England, but subsequent events shaped his thinking. He went on to become a committed preacher, wrestling with the relationship between church, state and monarch. This was an especially hot topic for Scots because after the Union of the Crowns, the monarchy tried to 'harmonise' religious observance and organisation across the United Kingdom by imposing Bishops on the Presbyterian Kirk. During the Reformation Protestantism replaced Roman Catholicism in England and Scotland, but only the Church of England acknowledged the monarch as head of its Church.

Samuel Rutherford questioned not only the monarchy's claim to be head of the Church but also its claim to rule by divine right. He believed there should be limits to the powers of any governing body or person. In his book *Lex, Rex (The Law and the King)* he wrote 'No person emerges from the womb in a state of civil subjugation to any king, prince or judge'. Dangerous views to voice let alone commit to paper!

Rutherford knew he risked arrest for treason, but at the time Charles I was occupied with a civil war in England. In Scotland, the Covenanters, denied freedom of worship by royal command, embarked on a military campaign, joining forces with those who believed in government by parliament. The conflict escalated into full blown civil war involving Scotland, England and Ireland during which Charles I lost his head. After 11 turbulent years of parliamentary rule however, the monarchy was restored in 1660, and Charles II had those he held responsible for the overthrow of the monarchy arrested. Samuel Rutherford was amongst them, but mercifully died before he could be tried. Copies of his book were publicly burned but Rutherford's ideas had already taken wing. By the end of the century limits had been put on the power of the monarchy and the principles he set out are enshrined in constitutions across the world. The words of a scholarly Teviotdale man reached far.

Other Ancrum folk were caught up in Charles II's campaign to eradicate the Covenanters. John Livingstone, Ancrum's minister, was deported for stirring up 'turbulency and sedition'. Like Rutherford, Livingstone's influence lived on: his great grandson Philip signed the United States of America's Declaration of Independence.

Return to A68 junction and turn left (signed Jedburgh).

Passing through Bonjedward, once the site of a castle and sizeable village, Monteviot House and Peniel Heugh behind are visible across the Teviot. On the right but not visible from this road are the ruins of Timpendean Tower. This tower, built on the edge of the royal hunting forest of Jedward, was a Douglas stronghold. This once mighty family owned extensive lands in the Tweed Dales. When Robert the Bruce's claim to the Scottish throne prevailed, he granted these lands to his loyal supporter James Douglas, he who honoured Bruce's unfulfilled wish by taking Bruce's heart on Crusade. Three centuries later however, Douglases had become such a threat to the monarchy that they were stripped of their land and titles. The wheel of royal patronage had come full circle.

Following now the Jed Water, the grand remains of Jedburgh Abbey rise above the trees as we round the bend and soon after we glimpse the 15th century tower house which briefly sheltered Mary Queen of Scots, with its adjacent orchard of ancient apple and pear trees.

Turn right into Canongate then left into carpark.

Jedburgh, known locally as Jethart, was originally called Jedward. In fact, there were two Jedwards, each with a church. However, David I established a priory in the northern Jedward in the early 12th century, elevated it to an abbey and gave the town Royal Burgh status; the other Jedward disappeared in all but name. Situated so close to the border, life here was unpredictable. The town was attacked so often that the Scots demolished the castle themselves in 1409 to prevent recapture by the English. But attacks continued and the town was occupied several times over the next 150 years. Even in peacetime, southbound traders arranged safe passage before they left Jedburgh.

The Abbey was attacked then abandoned in the middle of the 16th century. Somehow the church survived largely intact. Robert Allan, a native of Jedburgh, spoke for many awed by the effort and craft of building this impressive structure:

> *Thou massive pile, by massive spirits rear'd,*
> *Thy builders wrought*
> *Until their thought*
> *In beautiful, enduring stone appeared!*

In its heyday, the Abbey was just the place for a fairy tale royal wedding. And such a wedding took place in 1286 when widower Alexander III married Yolande, a French noblewoman. Like many a fairy tale though, things did not go quite as expected.

The Ghostly Wedding Guest

This wedding was to be no quiet affair. The great and the good of Scotland were invited to witness the marriage and join the celebrations. And there was much to celebrate! Yolande had captured a king no less and Alexander, who had no son, had hooked himself a young wife who would bear a new heir to the throne.

On the day, people flocked to the town to see their king and his new queen. The ceremony in the abbey went without a hiccup and the wedding party and their guests processed from the abbey up the hill to the castle for the wedding feast.

When the guests had eaten their fill, the court musicians soon had bride, groom and wedding guests whirling around the dance floor – until, that was, the dancers noticed a ghostly skeletal figure dancing amongst them. The musicians played on but the dancers, including the ghostly figure, who was later nowhere to be found, left the floor. Alexander shrugged off the incident as being of no consequence, but it had put a damper on the celebrations. Some thought it was a bad joke played by a would-be lover of the youthful Yolande. Others with a superstitious turn of mind thought it a bad omen.

And so indeed it proved to be. A few months later Alexander was dead. He and his horse fell from cliffs on the Fife coast while on an ill-advised night ride in stormy weather to see Yolande. It was a tragic accident presaged not only by the dancing wedding guest but, it was later claimed, by Thomas the Rhymer. The Rhymer, a contemporary of Alexander III, lived to witness the start of Scotland's ensuing troubles.

Bad luck alas befell Scottish royalty in Jedburgh a second time. Mary Queen of Scots came to Jedburgh to preside over a court but instead spent most of her time recovering from a fever developed after she and her horse fell into a bog. She had been visiting James Hepburn, Earl of Bothwell, who lay wounded at Hermitage Castle 20 miles to the south. He too recovered to become her third husband, but this marriage was not destined to last either: both died untimely deaths in other countries, he in Denmark, she in England. Mary was reported as saying later in her life 'Oh, that I had died at Jedburgh'. Her story is well told in the tower house which her loyal supporters, the Kerrs of Ferniehurst, had prepared for her. Not all Jedburgh's residents were as loyal: a messenger sent by Kerr with a proclamation of his loyalty to be read out at the market cross was met by a mob. They pulled him off his horse, dragged the proclamation from his hands and forced him to eat it.

Tensions within the community could of course run high for reasons besides religion and politics. The aftermath of one such instance in Jedburgh is the subject of a popular Border Ballad.

Rattlin' Willie

The inns and drinking howffs were filling up at the end of another market day in Jedburgh. And as usual, after a drink or two, out came the fiddles and the singing and dancing got going. At one of these merry gatherings Robin of

Sweetmilk Farm on nearby Rule Water and a local worthy called Willie got to arguing about which of them was the better fiddle player. The argument escalated and soon they were exchanging blows. Their fight ended when Willie, as well known for wielding a sword as a fiddle bow, stabbed and killed Robin.

A few weeks later, thinking he had got away with killing Robin, the gallus Willie turned up at Jedburgh Fair. However, he was spotted by Robin's friends, the Elliots. Intent on getting justice for their murdered friend, they waited until he left town at the end of the day and followed him.

> They followed him a' the way,
> They sought him up and down,
> In the links of Ousenam water
> They fund him sleeping sound.
>
> Stobs lighted aff his horse,
> And never a word he spak,
> Till he tied Willie's hands
> Fu' fast behind his back;
>
> Fu' fast behind his back,
> And down beneath his knee,
> And drink will be dear to Willie,
> When sweet milk gars him die.

Willie, who had consumed a fair amount of drink before he headed homeward, struggled unsuccessfully to get free. The Elliots, who had no doubt drunk a few themselves, resisted the temptation to avenge Robin's death there and then, but carried him back to Jedburgh to be locked up until he could be tried for murder. Justice for Robin of Sweetmilk was in the end done and seen to be done.

Exit car park, turn left and left again at T junction (signed Hawick).

The bulky outline of Jedburgh Castle gaol and museum dominates the skyline. The building, on the site of the town's medieval castle, was designed by John Howard, the 19th century reformer, and run as model prison. The Jedburgh of old however had a reputation for 'Jethart Justice', which was shorthand for hanging the accused first and asking questions after. This largely undeserved reputation was based on a 1547 case when the juror charged with reporting the jury's verdict, dozed off during the deliberations. When he woke up he pronounced 'Hang 'em aa!'.

A century and a half later in 1695, the last of many alleged witches to meet their death, a Jedburgh woman by the name of Shortreed, was burned on Beggarmuir. One of Jedburgh's earlier witch trials reveals that, by this time, the line between the world of witches and wizards, and that of fairies, which was quite distinct in the older tales, had become blurred.

The Witches of Jed

It was widely known in Jedburgh that Mr Brown the schoolteacher, a pious man, had a wife who gave him a hard time. His neighbours urged him to stand up to her, but he claimed she was a witch and he was afraid of 'her covine'. No one believed that of course. He was just one more hen-pecked husband and perhaps, they said, his fondness for drink merited the use of her sharp tongue. But then Brown was found dead in the river.

Rumours circulated in the wake of his death. Some claimed to have heard him pleading for divine help by singing the 23rd Psalm as he was dragged to the river by his wife and her associates. Others claimed to have seen fairies dancing on the top of Jedburgh Abbey that night, and some that the fairies had later been joined in their aerial dancing by the witches – and a local laird suspected of being a wizard. And what was more, they were drinking!

Word also went around the town that Mr Ainslie had gone into his cellar the next day to find that he was missing some bottles. And who else could have taken them but witches? Fairies would not do such a thing. Whatever the truth about Mr Ainslie's missing booze and how Mr Brown met his end, poor Mrs Brown was tried and found guilty of being a witch.

Still, long after the last witch trial the belief in witches continued. In 1752, when the army was recruiting in Jedburgh, one of the soldiers complained that his lodgings were haunted. He said that a ghostly apparition by his bed changed into a black cat, jumped out of the window and flew over the church steeple. He was, he told his captain, pretty sure the shape-shifting apparition was his landlady. The captain thought this unlikely but offered to keep vigil while the officer slept. So the next night, he lay awake with sword and pistol within reach, just in case. When a large black cat flew in through the window on the stroke of midnight, the captain grabbed his pistol, took aim and fired. Off flew the cat's ear and with a loud meow, it leapt out of the window.

The next morning the captain insisted on investigating what was under the landlady's cap. Finding her head swathed in bandages, he had them unwound till it was apparent she had lost her ear. He then threatened to have her arrested. Although being a witch or a wizard was no longer a capital crime, the poor woman did not want a prison term so she pleaded with him to keep her secret, if she promised never to use her powers again. This pledge he accepted but did not honour. How else would we know the story?

Jedburgh was the birthplace in the late 18th century of several men and women who, had they been born a few decades earlier might have been accused of being witches or wizards. Amongst them was a triumvirate of scientists who were to science what Walter Scott, James Hogg and their contemporaries were to literature. James Veitch was a physicist, astronomer, maker of telescopes, spectacles and clocks; Mary Somerville was a brilliant astronomer, mathematician, science writer and advocate of education and votes for women; and David Brewster was a specialist in optics whose inventions included the kaleidoscope.

Like other Border towns situated on rivers, Jedburgh had a textile industry, but was never a serious rival to neighbouring Hawick which had a faster flowing river. However, a government inspector of cloth reported in 1776 that Jedburgh lagged behind Melrose, Galashiels, Hawick and Kelso in producing hand-spun yarn and hand-woven cloth because 'there has been much dispute and discussion about their town's politics so that the people neglected all business and paid little or no attention to manufactures'. Like Kelso and Melrose, however, Jedburgh has been sustained by the legacy of its Abbey, and businesses serving the locality.

Return to A68 junction and turn right (signed Corbridge/Newcastle).

The Riddle of the Rocks

One day, a young man walking along the steep banks of the Jed Water at Inchbonny noticed that the red sandstone rocks exposed by the river were lying in horizontal layers on top of rocks of a different colour which were lying vertically. He recalled seeing something similar on the Berwickshire coast and worried away at this puzzle until he worked out the story these 'unconformities' were telling.

The man was James Hutton, later hailed as the father of modern geology. As we now know, the vertical strata are 430 million years old and had been tilted on their side before the horizontal rocks, a mere 370 million years old, came to rest on top. Hutton's concept of deep time stretching back hundreds of millions of years, and his statement 'I see no vestige of a beginning and no prospect of an end', had major ramifications not just for geology, science and history but also for theologians.

The story Hutton had to tell shook the very foundations of belief systems people had lived with for centuries, as did the work of a fellow Borderer, Robert Chambers. His anonymous *Vestiges of Creation* paved the way for Charles Darwin's revolutionary theory of evolution. Once again, the Scottish Borders had nurtured original genius!

James Hutton may have walked past the Capon Tree on the day he noticed the rocks. Oldest of the ancient trees that are the sole remains of Jedforest, the Capon is thought to be between 500 and 2,000 years old.

Passing the gates of Ferniehirst Castle, replete with colourful history but rarely open to the public, we meet the two 'r's Kerrs.

Kerypowed Handbaa

Dand (alias Andrew) Kerr is mentioned frequently in court proceedings in the turbulent 16th century. He survived the Battle of Flodden in 1513 and on the way home by Kelso cool-headedly installed his brother as the Commendator (CEO and Abbot in one) of Kelso Abbey. He forged alliances as suited the family interests and ambitions and, although Warden of the Middle March, he was himself a feared and fearless reiver.

Ferniehirst Castle, obscured then as now by trees, belonged to the 'kerypowed' (left handed) Kerrs who reversed the usual direction of the spiral staircases to give them the upper hand in defence. The castle, described by poet Walter Laidlaw as 'dour, grim and hoary' was besieged by Lord Dacre on the orders of Henry VIII of England in 1523. Laidlaw's poem 'The Siege' tells how, despite Dand's allies rushing to his aid, the castle was lost to the English and Dand taken prisoner. However, the locals crept back at night to cut loose the English horses and drive them, along with the herds of cattle waiting to grace the castle tables, into the woods.

Twenty years later Dand and his men pitched up at the Battle of Ancrum on the English side, but switched during the battle, an act that led to victory for the Scots. In the aftermath, the Kerrs lost Ferniehirst Castle again but, as another Laidlaw poem relates, got it back with help from the French. The Kerrs showed no mercy to their prisoners when they regained the castle. The story that the handbaa games, still played twice a year in Jedburgh, were originally played with the heads of English soldiers, is true.

Recited at the Jedburgh Common Riding, Laidlaw's poem ends,

> *The days of siege and raids are o'er,*
> *The din of war resounds no more;*
> *No sound except the song of bird*
> *Within the forest glade is heard.*

We leave the Kerrs on this peaceful note and head towards the upper reaches of the Teviot.

Turn right after gates of Ferniehurst Castle onto B6357 (signed Bonchester Bridge).

We climb past Lintalee, where the Black alias the Good Douglas ambushed and captured a troop of English soldiers with a handful of men and some birch branches, and continue past Swinnie Farm with views across to the Cheviots behind, until we crest the hill to descend into upper Teviotdale. The distinctive outlines of Ruberslaw and Black Law rise from the plain below.

At sign for Bedrule turn right onto single-track road with passing places.

Following the Rule Water between the Black Law and Ruberslaw past the ruin of Fulton Tower we reach Bedrule, a village visited in the past by medieval pilgrims and today by walkers on the Border Abbey Way. The church and the views from the churchyard are worth a detour (*follow sign to Bedrule Church*). The Turnbull family were given land here by the Good James Douglas in return for their loyalty.

A Tale of Two Bulls

Originally named Fairbairn, the family took the name Turnbull after one of them saved Robert the Bruce from being gored by an enraged bull. He grabbed its horns, turning it to the side just in time.

The Turnbull family had a reputation for unscrupulous reiving but also for producing prominent churchmen. Both Jedburgh and Melrose Abbeys had Abbot Turnbulls, and in the middle of the 15th century, William Turnbull, Bishop of Glasgow, persuaded James II, a distant relative, that Glasgow should have a university. James took the proposal to the Pope who in due course issued a papal bull founding the University of Glasgow, the fourth oldest university in the English-speaking world. And so, for a second time a bull featured in Turnbull family history!

Return to road, turn left and proceed towards Spital on Rule (continue straight on where, a mile or so beyond Bedrule, the road turns sharp right) and at junction with B6358 turn left (signed Hawick).

Approaching Spital of Rule, the eye is caught by the recently restored Fatlips Castle perched high on Minto Crags. For position and atmosphere this castle rivals Smailholm Tower. It was built by the Turnbulls but had passed to a branch of the Eliott family by the second half of the 17th century. They later became the Earls of Minto but, like the Kerrs or Kers, branches of this family distinguished themselves one from the other for reputational reasons by altering the spelling of their surname. A local verse explains which branch is associated with which place!

> *Double L and single T,*
> *Elliots of Minto and Wolflee;*
> *Double T and single L,*
> *The Eliotts they in Stobs that dwell;*
> *Single L and Single T,*
> *Eliots of St Germain they be;*
> *But double L and double T,*
> *The Deil may ken wha they may be.*

And the Devil, along with witches and fairies, was never far from the minds of the people of Teviotdale. As elsewhere in Scotland, it was thought that 'Rowan-tree and red threid/ Puts the witches to their speed'. The sight of cows with red thread tied around their horns to prevent them being milked by witches was common in Teviotdale. As for the fairies, some encounters were less alarming than others as Mrs Buckham, a Bedrule farmer's wife, discovered.

One Good Turn

One day Mrs Buckham was cooking bannocks with a heavy heart. It was the hungry time of year when food stores run low. Last year's harvest had been poor and there was hardly anything left in the meal kist. But the crops were still green in the fields and the berries were yet to ripen.

Just as she was wondering how they would feed their bairns when it was all gone, there was a chap at the door and in walked a small woman. She was dressed in green, which was not a fashionable look in Teviotdale at the time. Maybe though, thought Mrs Buckham, it is the height of fashion where she comes from.

Then the woman spoke. 'Can you spare a handful of meal... just the tiniest handful?' Well, Mrs Buckham had little enough but she couldn't see anyone starve so she went to the meal kist, scooped out a tiny handful, wrapped it in a wee bit of cloth and gave to the woman who thanked her and said, 'I will return what I have borrowed as soon as I can.'

When Mrs Buckram next went to the meal kist, she could see the bare wood at the bottom of it and knew their supply would not last the week. The very next day the little woman in green came again. This time Mrs Buckham was milking the cow and had her hands full. 'I see you're busy at the milking so I'll just pour the meal I borrowed into your meal kist', said the woman.

She did that and, as she left, said, 'For the help ye gied me, you'll have a bumper crop and prosper long.' And off she went.

Every night after that Mrs Buckham went to the meal kist expecting it to be the last time she would be able to scrape together enough for bannocks. But each night there was just enough for one more meal until the harvest was brought safely in and the meal kist filled to the brim. And, as the little woman in green had promised, it was a bumper harvest which would see them happily through the next hungry gap.

Mrs Buckham reaped a big reward for a small kindness to a stranger, but people went to great lengths to protect themselves from fairies with less benevolent intentions. Teviotdale folk believed that the blue bonnet of a new baby's father had to be kept at the mother's bedside to prevent the fairies switching their baby for a changeling. If the baby was taken before it was christened the fairies left a piglet in its place, but if the baby had been christened they left a bad-tempered imp. Just such a thing happened to a family at the foot of Minto Crags, but thanks to the minister, there was a happy ending.

The Baby and the Minister

The mother of a newly christened baby either forgot or did not believe in the local custom of keeping her husband's blue bonnet by their bed. One day, while she was working their small bit of land, she laid the sleeping baby by a bush. But when she came back to pick him up, there in her baby's place was a wee scrawny girning thing. Surely this was a changeling!

She scooped it up and ran off to ask the minister what was to be done. He told her to fetch some foxglove flowers, known locally as witches' thimbles. He would boil them up he said, give some of the liquid to this creature, scatter the boiled flowers on his body and wrap him up tight. Then she was to settle the wee thing in the cradle, shut and lock the door, give the key to the minister and come back in the morning.

The mother had doubts but brought the flowers, and the minister did all he had promised. He settled down to guard the door of the baby's room, and stayed there all night. And, as he told the worried mother when she came back in the morning, no one had entered or left the room. When he unlocked the door and brought out a healthy baby, the young mother was mightily relieved. Ever after, she made sure other women knew why it was necessary to keep their husband's blue bonnet beside their bed. However, it must have been a miracle the baby survived at all – the liquid the minister administered was laced with digitalis!

At junction with A698 turn left (signed Hawick) and proceed to Denholm.

Somewhere on this stretch of the Teviot, St Cuthbert and a young lad once went fishing.

St Cuthbert and the Eagle

Cuthbert, like his predecessor Boisil, often left the monastery at Old Mailros for days and weeks at a time to go into the valleys and hills of the Tweed. His mission was to take the Christian message to the people and to baptise those he converted.

On these journeys, Cuthbert was given food and shelter by people he met along the way, but on this occasion, he and his young companion came across an eagle killing a large fish on the banks for the Teviot. The boy accompanying Cuthbert ran to pick up the fish for their dinner. Cuthbert, however, stayed his hand and insisted they give half to the eagle, whose labour had caught it. He also insisted that they share their half with some strangers who happened to be walking on that stretch of the river.

Denholm is an ancient settlement but the village we see today is a 'planned village', a rarity in the Borders. Land was granted in the late 17th and 18th centuries for the explicit purpose of building houses and gardens laid out on an orderly fashion around not one but two village greens. It was an agricultural village until, late in the 18th century, Denholm embraced the stocking knitting frame. In the 19th century demand for local stone for houses and mills in Hawick also generated jobs.

This one village nurtured several talented people who made major contributions to their fields. They include John Scott, a botanist who corresponded with Darwin, and James Murray, first editor of the Oxford English Dictionary. There were so many James Murrays in Teviotdale that this one 'adopted' two middle names to make life easier for the postman. Denholm was also the birthplace of John Leyden, the poet and orientalist who predated and inspired them all.

Exit Denholm and turn second left onto minor road (signed Cavers).

John Leyden described the scene as the road skirts the western slopes of Ruberslaw:

> *Dark Ruberslaw that lifts his head sublime,*
> *Rugged and hoary with the wrecks of time*
> *On his broad misty front the giant wears*
> *The horrid furrows of ten thousand years.*

Ruberslaw, like the Eildons, has volcanic origins and is associated with folklore the origins of which, like the hilltop, are frequently shrouded in mist. Leyden spent his childhood here and was adept at reading the landscape. By the time he died in Java at the age of 36, he had qualified as a minister, re-trained as a doctor, and written some fine poetry. Descriptions of his boyhood haunts, their history and the emotions the landscape evoked run through his poems, like 'Scenes of Infancy'.

> *Is that dull sound the hum of Teviot's stream?*
> *Is that blue light the moon's or tomb-fire's gleam,*
> *By which a mouldering pile is faintly seen,*
> *The old deserted church of Hazeldean,*
>
> *Where slept my fathers in their natal clay,*
> *Till Teviot's waters roll'd their bones away?*
> *Their feeble voices from the stream they raise,*
> *"Rash youth! unmindful of thy early days,*
> *Why didst thou quit the peasant's simple lot?*
> *Why didst thou leave the peasant's turf-built cot,*
> *The ancient graves, where all thy fathers lie,*
> *And Teviot's stream, that long has murmured by?*

Leyden collaborated with Sir Walter Scott on his *Minstrelsy of the Scottish Borders* and, like James Hogg, was not one to conform to polite society. 'Rough diamonds' from humble stock, they both related to the physical world in a way that those who had less direct contact with the land in their early years, or perhaps less freedom to explore, could. John Leyden was not, however, the only local poet. James Thomson's famous poem 'Winter' was inspired by the sight of a storm on the Ruberslaw. Its moods were a weather vane for the local population:

> *When Ruberslaw puts on his cowl,*
> *The Dunion on his hood,*
> *Then a' the wives in Teviotdale,*
> *Ken there will be a flood.*

Moody Ruberslaw helped the locals out of tight spots on at least one occasion. When, during 'the Killing Times' of the 1680s, a watchman alerted a secret gathering of Covenanters that the local militia were on their way, the quick-thinking minister prayed that God would cover them with his cloak. Immediately a Ruberslaw mist descended and everyone made good their escape. Religious radicalism was widespread here: Thomas Boston and Thomas Chalmers preached as did Alexander Peden, a well-known travelling Covenanter, who spoke to a large crowd from a rocky platform on Ruberslaw, afterwards known as Peden's Pulpit.

Cavers was once a sizeable town which explains its now incongruously large church. The kirkyard looks up and down Teviotdale. There is also an unusual statue which was originally in the garden of Cavers House. William Leggat was a local lad who became a 'weel-kent' figure as a jack-of-all-trades running messages for Lady Cavers. A stone mason at Cavers quarry made the likeness, but Willie took exception to his graven image and kicked it, so removing his dog's left ear! Willie died in the 18th century but the statue was recently rescued and restored by local craftsmen, still minus the ear.

At T junction with A6088 turn right, at junction with A698 turn left (signed Hawick), proceed to Hawick and follow signs for Town Centre and parking.

The grand and not so grand 19th century buildings in Hawick High Street reflect its relatively late and piecemeal development as a town.

> *Boast! Hawick, boast! thy structures reared in blood,*
> *Shall rise triumphant over flame and flood.*

These lines from Hawick's town song sum up the challenges the town faced in its early days. Growing from humble beginnings, it had a castle but no abbey and was not a royal burgh, although Mary Queen of Scots gave it 110 houses and a baronial charter. Many such burghs of Barony did not endure but Hawick, despite its proximity to the border and proneness to attack, somehow did. On one occasion when the town was set alight by English troops, the only building to survive was Drumlanrig Tower, now the Border Textile Tower and Museum at the end of the High Street.

Situated at the confluence of the Slitrig and the Teviot, the town was prone to flooding. Local historian Alexander Jeffrey described the Slitrig as 'wild and unruly' and Leyden as 'black haunted Slata'. A devastating flash flood in 1767 was thought by some to have been caused by fairies living beside a pool near the river's source. A stone cast into the pool by a passing human upset them, prompting a torrent in retaliation.

It was though the wildness of the Slitrig that proved to be Hawick's best asset. Perfectly suited to powering textile machinery, it enabled the meteoric rise of an industry which increased the population to 17,000 by 1970. By the middle of the 19th century, around four fifths of Scotland's stocking knitting frames were in the Borders, and half of these were in Hawick. Hawick alone produced more than one million pairs of stockings a year. Mill owners had to be alert to changes in fashion however. They adapted to men giving up breeches in favour of trousers by moving production into fine woollen underwear and socks. Later, when new fabrics came to dominate the underwear market, they used underwear designs to make outerwear which became the height of fashion. As James Thomson of Bowden wrote in his poem 'The Auld Mid Raw',

> *This life is but a shiftin' scene,*
> *The world gaes circlin' roun',*
> *And Time's brought mony changes*
> *To oor ain auld toon.*
> *New fashions tak' the causa' croon,*
> *The auld gae to the wa'.*

And, as Isabella Johnstone's poem 'Border Weaver' comments,

> *And oh! The stuff she's asked tae weave,*
> *Fair makes her blush tae think o't*

But it's what they want ayont the seas
Americans an' what not...
She's like a guid bit tweed herself
Made tae lest forever,
And wearin weel, ye couldna tell
The storms she's had tae weather.

The production of textiles on an industrial scale however came at a price. When he visited, John Ruskin despaired of the level of pollution saying 'I know finally what value the British mind sets on the beauties of nature'. Thankfully, later technological advances and regulation improved the situation over time.

Hawick has never forgotten its pre-industrial past. Each year at the Common Riding the triumphs of Hawick's fighting men are recalled. The inclusion in the town's song of the line 'Aye defend your rights of Common' has particular significance to the people of Hawick, as does the ritual of riding the marches. Over the centuries, Hawick has successfully defended its common lands from encroachment most recently in a landmark legal case. The court awarded the Duke of Buccleuch 30 per cent of the contested land he claimed, confirming the rest as common land for the people of Hawick.

Leaving Hawick, follow signs for A7 and turn left onto A7 south (signed Langholm/ Carlisle).

Beyond Goldielands Tower we come to Branxholm Tower, the main 15th century residence of the branch of the Scotts from which the Dukes of Buccleuch are descended. It was one of countless Border strongholds destroyed in the mid-16th century. The Scotts however had the resources and will to rebuild Branxholm, and in later more peaceable times adapted it to modern styles. As Sir Walter Scott's lines from the Lay of the Last Minstrel illustrate, Scott of Buccleuch was able to rally huge numbers of men to fight for the Scott cause:

Nine-and-twenty knights of fame
Hung their shields in Branxholm Hall;
Nine-and-twenty squires of name
Brought them their steeds to bower from stall
Nine-and-twenty yeoman tall
Waited duteous on them all;
They were all knights of mettle true
Kinsmen to the bold Buccleuch.

It was from Branxholm that 'the bold Buccleuch' coordinated the rescue of Kinmont Willie from prison in Carlisle in 1596, and later the return of stolen cattle to Jamie Telfer. Both events are immortalised in classic Border Ballads.

Bold Buccleuch to the rescue

Kinmont Willie was Willie Armstrong who had undoubtedly committed the offences he was charged with. Leading 'Kinmont's Bairns', he carried out raids across the border returning with herds of cattle and other booty. It was inevitable that he would be called to account if not killed first. The trouble was that Kinmont Willie had been arrested on the Scottish side of the Border on a truce day.

Now word has gane tae the bauld keeper,
In Branksome Ha', where that he lay,
That Lord Scroope has ta'en the Kinmont Willie,
Between the hours of night and day.

And here detained him, Kinmont Willie,
Against the truce of Border tide.
And forgotten that the bauld Buccleuch
Is keeper on the Scottish side?

This was a serious breach of the March Laws. Scott was the Scottish Warden of the March and as such responded in a measured way, determined to right an injustice. As the ballad relates he did not set out to take Carlisle Castle, simply to liberate Kinmont Willie,

'But since nae war's between the lands,
And here is peace, and peace should be;
I will neither harm English lad or lass,
And yet the Kinmont shall be free.'

Mission accomplished, he and his men set off home with Kinmont Willie. Lord Scrope, who was responsible for the castle and its prisoners, then responded in a less measured way, pursuing Scott and the rescued Willie over the Scottish Border where he added insult to diplomatic injury by burning towns and villages, and seizing more prisoners to be marched back to Carlisle. Thankfully Queen Elizabeth took a dim view of Scrope's actions and the Scottish nobles agreed to let it go.

It was Scott of Branxholm to the rescue again when English reivers attacked Jamie Telfer's house and took away the few cattle he possessed. This ballad, 'Jamie Telfer o' the Fair Dodhead', throws light on the network of alliances Border families formed for their mutual protection, and how ties of obligation to those who were not 'kin' were built up.

After an attack in his house, Jamie ran over the hills to Stob's Hall on the banks of the Slitrig in the hills below Hawick. This was the home of Gibbie Elliot who, when Jamie told him what had happened, replied,

'Gar seek your succour at Branksome Ha',
For succour ye'se get nane frae me!
Gae seek your succour where ye paid black mail,
For man! ye ne'er paid money to me.'

Elliot's denial that Jamie had paid black mail (protection money) to him was a blow, but he ran on to his brother-in-law's house who, although he could do little himself to help, gave Jamie a horse. On he rode to William Wat's. He sent his sons out to saddle their horses and off they rode with Jamie.

And whan they cam to Branksome Ha',
They shouted a' baith loud and hie,
Till up and spak him auld Buccleuch,
Said—'Whae's this brings the fray to me?'

> 'It's I, Jamie Telfer o' the fair Dodhead,
> And a harried man I think I be!
> There's nought left in the fair Dodhead,
> But a greeting wife, and bairnies three'.

Buccleuch honoured his obligation to protect Jamie by gathering men to pursue the English raiding party and retrieve Jamie Telfer's kye (cattle). And returned they were – with interest. The ten stolen kye had become thirty-three!

Pressing south towards Teviothead, we get a sense of how challenging these journeys through the hills in all weathers must have been for men and their mounts.

At Teviothead turn right onto minor road (signed Carlenrig and Merrylaw) to Teviothead Church.

Teviothead is close to Liddesdale and to the border with England. It is also where the fearless Border reiver Johnnie Armstrong was ambushed when he accepted an invitation to go hunting with the 17-year-old King James V. Johnnie's version of events is the subject of another famous ballad.

Johnnie Armstrong

Johnnie turns up to meet his king in his finest clothes and with an entourage. But as he pledges his allegiance to James, he realises that the king intends to kill him. Johnnie offers all sorts of inducements to be let go free, but to each of these the king replies,

> 'Away, away, thou traitor strang!
> Out o' my sight soon mayst thou be!
> I grantit never a traitor's life,
> And now I'll not begin with thee.'

Johnnie's dignified reply is,

> *'Ye lied, ye lied, now, King,' he says,*
> *'Altho' a King and Prince ye be!*
> *For I've luved naething in my life,*
> *I weel dare say it, but honesty –*

Then, realising that the king was not going to relent,

> *'To seik het waater beneath cauld ice,*
> *Surely it is a greit folie–*
> *I have asked grace at a graceless face,*
> *But there is nane for my men and me!'*

Johnnie and his men were killed and dumped unceremoniously in a pit. The site, just before the church, is marked and the story told on information boards. A memorial stone in the churchyard also commemorates Johnnie, a charismatic leader and self-made man who was styled 'King of the Borders' by those who admired him, and as a rogue by those who did not.

The back story of this ballad explains the special place its episode has in Border history. Other than the king, and those without land or employment, everyone in the rural Borders was obligated to and dependent on people above and below them. Although Johnnie Armstrong gained his wealth and power by the dubious means of extorting 'black mail', he had signed a bond of 'man rent' with the Maxwell family pledging to support them in war and peace – in return for their protection. By acknowledging Maxwell as his superior, Johnnie no doubt thought he had positioned himself in the social order legitimately. In the eyes of James v, however, he was flaunting the royal rule that his patronage alone determined who had wealth and influence.

James v probably believed that eliminating Johnnie would gain him the respect and support of Scotland's nobility as well as pleasing his English uncle, Henry viii. How wrong he was! Tricking Armstrong was acceptable, but killing him and his men signalled that the king thought himself above the law – exactly the kind of behaviour he wanted the Border Reivers to give up! This was not the way to win the confidence of the nobility and stamp out reiving.

Return to A7, turn left to continue towards Hawick and, just beyond Branxholm Castle, turn left (signed Chapelhills). The single-track road with passing places requires two stops to open and close gates. (For an alternative route, continue on A7 north, turn left onto B711 (signed Roberton) and turn right at sign for Harden/ Borthwickshiels to rejoin route).

Heading west, this road offers superb views to east, west, north and south. Tiny Chisholm on the descent is named for a family who performed a similar feat to the Turnbulls. This time the king was saved from attack by a wild boar. Skirting the Craik Forest, the road descends to the Borthwick Water, crosses it, and follows the river.

At junction with B711 turn right (signed Hawick), pass through Roberton and turn onto single-track road with passing places (signed Harden/ Borthwickshiels).

Journeying up this valley takes us to the very heart of reiver country and to Harden, the later home Auld Wat Scott and Mary the Flower of Yarrow. This fortress came with an outdoor larder which was replenished periodically with plundered cattle. When supplies ran low Mary would serve her husband a dish of spurs to signal that he should gather his men and fetch a fresh supply of beef. Wat and Mary had six sons and six daughters not to mention retainers and visitors, so no doubt he was served the spurs quite often. Poet Will Ogilvie, captures the spirit of the Scotts of Harden and their moonlight reiving;

> *There are more than birds on the hill tonight,*
> *And more than winds on the plain!*
> *The threat of the Scotts has filled the moss,*
> *'There will be moonlight again.'*
> *Ho! for the blades of Harden!*
> *Ho! for the ring of steel!*
> *The stolen steers of a hundred years*
> *Come home for a Kirkhope meal!*

Harden has quick access to Ettrick, Yarrow and Teviotdale but was a perfect hideaway. As John Leyden's lines in 'Scenes of Infancy,' describe,

> *Where Bortha (Borthwick) hoarse, that loads the meads with sand,*
> *Rolls her red tide to Teviot's western strand,*
> *Through slaty hills, whose sides are shagg'd with thorn,*
> *Where springs in scattered tufts the dark green corn,*
> *Towers wood-girt Harden, far above the vale,*
> *And clouds of ravens o'er the turrets sail;*
> *A hardy race, who never shrunk from war,*
> *The Scott, to rival realms a mighty bar,*
> *Here fixed his mountain home—a wide domain.*

Still in private hands, the house is now ably defended by fierce road humps on the approach – so visit with care.

217

Auld Wat was infamous for some less savoury exploits but famous, if the ballads are to be believed, for leadership and principled actions. He was a man of his time and place, and the essence of the reiving spirit ran through his veins. Wat's bugle horn with episodes from his life carved into the handle now sits in the Museum of Scotland in Edinburgh.

Turn right at T junction (signed Ashkirk) and proceed to Ashkirk.

With glorious views in front and behind us, the bleak otherworldly beauty of this upland landscape unfolds. As the road starts to descend to the Ale Water, ridges of white rock gleam and sheep march stoically along well-trodden paths. A roadside monument to the life and poetry of Will Ogilvie is fittingly located on the route that inspired his poem the 'Hill Road to Roberton' tracing a journey down the road we have just travelled:

The hill road to Roberton: Ale Water at our feet,
And grey hills and blue hills that melt away and meet,
With cotton-flowers that wave to us and lone whaups that call,
And over all the Border mist – the soft mist overall.

When Scotland married England long, long ago,
The winds spun a wedding-veil of moonlight and snow
A veil of filmy silver that sun and rain had kissed,
And she left them to the Border in a soft grey mist,

And now the dreary distance doth wear it like a bride,
Out beyond the Langhope Burn and over Essenside,
By Borthwick Wa's and Redfordgreen and on to wild Buccleugh,
And up the Ettrick Water, till it fades into the blue.

The winding road to Roberton is little marked of wheels,
And lonely past Blawearie runs the track to Borthwickshiels,
Whitslade is slumbering undisturbed and down in Harden Glen,
The tall trees murmur in their dreams of Wat's mosstrooping men.

A distant glint of silver, that is Ale's last goodbye,
Then Greatmoor and Windburgh against the purple sky,
The long line of the Carter, Teviotdale flung wide,
As a slight stir in the heather – a wind from the English side.

The hill road to Roberton's a steep road to climb,
But where your foot has crushed it, you can smell the scented thyme,
And if your heart's a Border heart, look down on Harden Glen,
And hear the blue hills ringing with the restless hooves again.

Passing through Ashkirk, at junction with A7 turn left (signed Galashiels) then right onto B6400 (signed Lilliesleaf).

The managed landscape of mixed arable pastoral farms here is the product of the agricultural improvements of the 18th and 19th centuries. Prior to that, the land between here and the Eildons had many fortified towers. Lilliesleaf was once crammed with hand spinners and handweavers but shrank when textile production was mechanised and workers gravitated to Galashiels and Hawick.

At T junction in Lilliesleaf turn left onto B6350, follow signs for Melrose to sign for Bowden and turn right onto B6398 (signed Bowden/ Newtown St Boswells).

Bowden, like Lilliesleaf, was once a much larger village. A memorial in the church remembers Lady Grizzell Baillie whose pious zeal and championing of public health as well as the rights of women and children, made her the first deaconess of the Church of Scotland. The 19th century missionary and social reformer, Mary Slessor also lived here with her adopted Nigerian children whilst recovering from illness. Amongst her adopted children were twins who, due to local Nigerian belief, would have otherwise been killed. She worked tirelessly to eradicate such superstitions while respecting African culture as a whole knowing that it was not that long since comparable superstitions blighted the lives of Borderers.

Bowden, tucked in below the southernmost Eildon, had its share of superstition as Thomas Wilkie, a medical student and one Sir Walter Scott's collectors for *Minstrelsy of the Scottish Borders*, knew well. Wilkie reported a local belief that, just as everyone had a guardian angel who could save their life, everyone also had a 'thrumpin', which had the power to end it. And he was told that on 'Cowlug E'en', sprites with lugs (ears) like cows appeared. Curiously, no one could tell him on what night of the year Cowlug E'en fell. Perhaps his informant was having a laugh at his expense. Or was Wilkie, who lived in Bowden for a time, teasing Scott?

The Wag at the Waa

Wilkie also noted down a local rhyme about the 'Wag-at-the-Waa', a character who frequented Border kitchens. The Wag at the Waa was a tiny wizened old man with a tail who took up residence beside the fire, or, if there was no cooking pot hanging on the iron hook, over the fire in the crook of the hook. Like the brownies, he would only leave if a family member died or offended him by paying him for work done.

The trouble was that the Wag at the Waa did not do much work. Instead he took pleasure in tormenting the servants. Once he was up on the crook it was quite a business getting him to give up his seat so pots could be hung on and swung over the fire to cook. Word got around that cutting a cross into the crook of the hook for the pots stopped them taking up residence on the crook, and eventually Wag at the Waas disappeared from Border kitchens. Well into the 20th century however, children were warned not to wag the crook lest the Wag at the Waa jumped on!

Here at the back of the Eildon Hills we reach the end of our journeys. We give the final words to Andrew Lang – his personal tribute to Scott and the landscape he also made his own.

St Boswell's golf course

Three crests against a saffron sky
Beyond the purple plain,
The kind remembered melody
Of Tweed once more again
Like a loved ghost thy fabled flood
Fleets through the dusky land;
Where Scott, come home to die, has stood,
My feet returning stand.
A mist of memory broods and floats,
The Border waters flow,
The air is full of ballad notes
Borne out of long ago.
Twilight and Tweed and Eildon Hill,
Fair and too fair you be;
You tell me that the voice is still
That should have welcomed me.

Return to B6398 /B6359 junction, turn right (signed Melrose) and follow signs to Tweedbank Station.

Timeline

6000–3000 BCE
Mesolithic — Nature worshipping hunter gatherers.

3500–1750 BCE
Neolithic — Sky worshipping early farmers (standing stones and circles).

1750–700 BCE
Bronze Age — Element worshipping (earth fire water) field farmers (hill top gathering places).

700 BCE–80 CE
Iron Age — Celtic British farming tribes: defended settlements; hill top gathering places.

80–220 CE — Episodic Roman rule over Celtic British tribes.

220–600 CE — Celtic British tribes Selgovae, Votadini and Gadeni control territories.

From 600 CE — Anglo Saxon rule as part of Kingdom of Bernicia later expanded to become Kingdom of Northumbria: kin alliances; Christianity spreads from early abbeys and priories (St Cuthbert; St Kentigern /Mungo) to challenge ancient beliefs (Merlin); English replaces Cymric.

850–1018 CE — Unification of Scottish Kingdoms of Picts, Strathclyde and Lothians, Lauderdale and Wedale. Other Tweed dales remain part of Kingdom of Northumbria.

From late 1000s CE — Normans take control of and reform Kingdom of Northumbria: feudal landholding; burghs /towns; parishes; new abbeys; (King David I); Roman Catholicism prevails but popular belief in magic, prophecy and other worlds persists (Michael Scot).

1270s–1314 CE	Independence threatened but retained (William Wallace; King Robert the Bruce); Battle of Flodden 1314; Roman Catholicism co-exists with superstition and belief in prophecy and fairies (Thomas the Rhymer).
1314–1500s CE	Ongoing English / Scottish battle for control of land between Tweed and Cheviot Hills; tower houses; Border Reivers.
1500s CE	Decline of the Monasteries/The Scottish Reformation: Scottish Presbyterianism replaces Roman Catholicism (John Knox); 'The rough wooing' (Mary Queen of Scots; Henry VIII of England).
1600s CE	1603 Union of the Crowns (James VI Scotland /James I of England); political and religious dissent (Covenanters); witch-hunts; 'War of the Three Nations' (royalists vs parliamentarians): Charles I deposed – Commonwealth Rule 1649 – 1660; Restoration (restoration Charles II); 1685 Jacobite rebellion.
1700s CE	1707 Union of Scottish and English Parliaments: religious and political dissent; Jacobite rebellions 1715 and 1745; agricultural revolution; expansion of hand produced textile industry; Lowland Clearances; Scottish Enlightenment.
1800s CE	First Industrial Revolution: mechanisation of textile manufacturing processes: factories; factory towns; railways; tourism; literary boom (Walter Scott, James Hogg).
1900s–present	World Wars I and II; textile boom and bust; growth and collapse of electronics industry; literary boom continues (John Buchan: Borders Book Festival); expansion leisure and tourism; Waverley Railway line reopens 2015.

Luath Press Limited
committed to publishing well written books worth reading

LUATH PRESS takes its name from Robert Burns, whose little collie Luath (*Gael.,* swift or nimble) tripped up Jean Armour at a wedding and gave him the chance to speak to the woman who was to be his wife and the abiding love of his life. Burns called one of 'The Twa Dogs' Luath after Cuchullin's hunting dog in Ossian's *Fingal*. Luath Press was established in 1981 in the heart of Burns country, and now resides a few steps up the road from Burns' first lodgings on Edinburgh's Royal Mile. Luath offers you distinctive writing with a hint of unexpected pleasures.

Most bookshops in the UK, the US, Canada, Australia, New Zealand and parts of Europe either carry our books in stock or can order them for you. To order direct from us, please send a £sterling cheque, postal order, international money order or your credit card details (number, address of cardholder and expiry date) to us at the address below. Please add post and packing as follows: UK – £1.00 per delivery address; overseas surface mail – £2.50 per delivery address; overseas airmail – £3.50 for the first book to each delivery address, plus £1.00 for each additional book by airmail to the same address. If your order is a gift, we will happily enclose your card or message at no extra charge.

Luath Press Limited
543/2 Castlehill
The Royal Mile
Edinburgh EH1 2ND
Scotland
Telephone: 0131 225 4326 (24 hours)
email: sales@luath.co.uk
Website: www.luath.co.uk